THE SHORT GAME MAGIC OF TIGER WOODS

Also by John Andrisani

The Tiger Woods Way:
An Analysis of Tiger Woods'
Power-Swing Technique

THE SHORT GAME MAGIC OF TIGER WOODS

AN ANALYSIS OF TIGER WOODS' PITCHING, CHIPPING, SAND PLAY, AND PUTTING TECHNIQUES

BY

JOHN ANDRISANI

THREE RIVERS PRESS   NEW YORK

Copyright © 1998 by John Andrisani

Published by Three Rivers Press, a division of Crown Publishers, Inc.,
201 East 50th Street, New York, New York 10022.
Member of the Crown Publishing Group.

Random House, Inc. New York, Toronto, London, Sydney, Auckland
www.randomhouse.com

THREE RIVERS PRESS is a registered trademark
of Random House, Inc.

Originally published in hardcover by
Crown Publishers, Inc., in 1998.

First paperback edition published by
Three Rivers Press in 1999.

Printed in the United States of America

Design by June N. Karen

Library of Congress Cataloging-in-Publication Data

Andrisani, John.
The short game magic of Tiger Woods : an analysis of
Tiger Woods' pitching, chipping, sand play, and
putting techniques / by John Andrisani.—1st ed.
Includes index.
1. Short game (Golf). 2. Woods, Tiger. I. Title.
GV979.S54A53   1998
796.352'3—dc21   98–10494

ISBN 0-609-80420-0

10   9   8   7   6   5   4   3   2   1

First Paperback Edition

CONTENTS

*The secrets to scoring are letting your
imagination run wild and learning Tiger's
creative swing techniques.*

*Reading the lie correctly, knowing when to
give the ball more air time than ground
time—or vice versa—and alternating between
a wristless and a wristy stroke are Tiger's vital
strategies for hitting the ball close to the cup.*

*Knowing on what path to swing the club
and how far to hit behind the ball are critical
links to playing basic and more sophisticated
sand shots like Tiger.*

*Learning Tiger's pure pendulum stroke will
help you sink more long, short, and curling
putts.*

ACKNOWLEDGMENTS

First and foremost, I thank the golf enthusiasts who bought the first book I wrote on Tiger, *The Tiger Woods Way*. I also thank my agent Scott Waxman and Steve Ross of Crown Publishers, Inc.

I'm grateful to Sue Carswell, my editor at Crown, who stayed on top of things from start to finish, as did her assistant, Rachel Kahan. Also, special thanks to Walter Heffernan.

My hat is also off to all of those talented people who helped enhance the book's visual elements. Kudos to artist Allen Welkis for his outstanding lifelike drawings of Tiger. Thanks also to Phil Sheldon and Jan Traylen of England for their wonderful Tiger "takes."

I thank all of the teachers and Tour pros for their keen insights on what makes Tiger's innovative short game techniques tick.

As usual, my personal typist, Patti Bills, was there for me, at all hours of the day and night.

I thank my friends for forgiving me for not spending quality time with them—on and off the course.

I'm also grateful to all those responsible for helping Tiger develop a supreme short game, particularly his father, Earl, personal coach Claude "Butch" Harmon, and pro John Anselmo.

INTRODUCTION

I don't know who said, "Star quality is that little something extra," but I do know that it applies to Tiger Woods' short game.

Tiger is, of course, known best for his power game, both off the tee and from the fairway. In fact, in my book *The Tiger Woods Way*, I analyzed the secrets of his power-swing technique and provided additional commentary from the game's most renowned teachers and professional players.

Even if you are a new golfer, you realize that power alone will not get you through a day on the links. To shoot the scores you dream about, you must be able to hit good pitch shots, chips, sand shots, and putts.

Over the years, there have been some great short game players. Going back in time to the 1920s, Walter Hagen could sure get the ball up and in from almost anywhere around the greens. Bobby Jones was pretty darn talented, too. In fact, his greenside prowess played a big role in his 1930 Grand Slam win. In the decades that followed, from the 1940s through the 1980s, Bobby Locke, Ken Venturi, Arnold Palmer, Gary Player, Chi Chi Rodriguez, Tom Watson, and Seve Ballesteros were recognized as the best touch players. Among the younger players on the PGA Tour to emerge in the 1990s, there was no match for Phil Mickelson—until Tiger Woods came along.

Golf experts recognize Tiger as one of the game's premier short game players. "When he's on, nobody can touch him around or on the greens," says Gary Player.

It's one thing that Tiger can spin the ball into the hole with a pitching wedge, chip balls in with a three wood, hole sand shots from buried lies, and sink long breaking putts from the other side of a green. It's another thing that he performs well under pressure—which brings me to the essence of a good short game.

To hit clutch short game shots, you must employ different swings that are so practiced they almost operate on automatic pilot once you take the club away. In Tiger's case, his pitching, chipping, sand play, and putting techniques are so fundamentally sound that they stand up under the heat of competition.

You must also be able to look at a lie and read it; in short, to know which club will work best and precisely what the ball will do in the air and on the ground. You must also be mentally creative enough to see yourself play a good shot before you swing. This imagery enhances your confidence, so that you can make a tension-free, technically correct swing. It also helps you determine how hard to hit the ball.

This same kind of preswing procedure is vital on the greens. Tiger is very good at reading the break in greens and judging speed, which are two reasons why he sinks so many putts. In winning the 1994, 1995, and 1996 U.S. Amateur titles and his first major title as a professional, the 1997 Masters at Augusta National

Golf Club, it seemed he made every putt he looked at. And, in case you didn't know it, he never three-putted once on Augusta's treacherous sloping greens.

There is no doubt that Tiger is a genius, but he wasn't born a superb short game player. He built this talent through hard, imaginative practice, inventing new shots all his life—starting in childhood when he taught himself how to hit the quick-stopping long bunker shot. He was so creative, he practiced hitting wedge shots over the dorms at Stanford and putting on the university's gymnasium floor. That's dedication.

By learning the ins and outs of Tiger's pitching, chipping, sand play, and putting methods, you too can learn to save shots. In *The Short Game Magic of Tiger Woods,* I'll provide you with an in-depth analysis of Tiger's preswing procedure and include both setup and swing keys. Additionally, you'll be shown how to hit trouble shots and groove your game by working on simple drills.

If you'll let me pat myself on the back, I'd say the advantage of this short game book over others—aside from analyzing one of golf's most creative short game players—is its simplicity. The instructions are written as straightforwardly as possible, with accompanying illustrations and photographs that make the message come through even more clearly. I prepared the book this way to show respect for Tiger's easy-to-repeat techniques. I want you to be able to learn shots quickly, so you can go straight to the course and try them.

Good luck in your quest to become a pro-type short game player.

JOHN ANDRISANI

THE SHORT GAME MAGIC OF TIGER WOODS

1

PITCHING MAGIC

The secrets to scoring are letting your imagination run wild and learning Tiger's creative swing techniques.

Whenever I watch a pro hitting a variety of pitch shots during a round of golf, I'm reminded of the late Louis Armstrong, who, just by blowing more gently or forcefully into his trumpet and hitting different valves with varying degrees of pressure, was able to produce hundreds of sounds.

It's fair to say that Tiger Woods is a very musical player. He creates many different pitch shots by moving the ball around in his stance; positioning his feet differently; altering his grip pressure; changing the angle and tempo of his swing; and using any one of three wedges.

The pitching wedge, sand wedge, and lob wedge normally feature 52, 56, and 60 degrees of loft, respectively. In addition to being very lofted, all of these clubs are short, feature heavier heads than the other irons, and are more upright. Because of these features they are far easier to swing and control than the longer, less lofted clubs—for Tiger and the average golfer.

I can understand why you may have some trouble learning and mastering the driver swing. But there's no excuse for not becoming a good wedge player, especially if you copy Tiger's simpler methods and devote just a little bit of time to practice. As Sam Snead once told me in 1986, when I met with him in Helsinki, Finland, where he was giving a midnight teaching exhibition: "Practicing wedges in the fifty- to hundred-yard range is the best way to get a feel for each club and learn the length of backswing required for a specific length shot."

Understandably, you would rather go out and hit a few buckets of balls at the driving range than practice pitch shots. But if you are really serious about lowering your handicap and reaching your true potential as a player, you must learn to play the wedges. After all, if you can pitch the ball close to the hole, from out in the fairway or close by the green, you'll be more likely to save par when an errant drive gets you into trouble or to score birdie on either short par-4 holes or par 5s.

When it comes to hitting full pitching wedge shots and part shots with the sand wedge and 60-degree lob wedge, Tiger truly is in a class of his own—and not just because of the simplicity of his swing, either. Tiger has an uncanny ability to read a lie, judge distance, choose a technique that matches the weather and course conditions, and know where the clubhead is at different points in the swing. Further, Tiger's pitching game was founded on the basics. Therefore, his techniques are far easier to repeat over and over again than the more unorthodox methods typically used by superb self-taught wedge players such as Seve Ballesteros and Chi Chi Rodriguez. Unlike them, Tiger learned the basics from his father, Earl, and by studying under California teacher John Anselmo from the ages of ten to seventeen.

Although Tiger was nurtured in the fundamentals, club-level golfers can learn a lot about creative shot making from Tiger. That's because he's always taught himself new shots by hitting balls out of different lies with different clubs. Moreover, since 1993, Tiger has studied under Claude "Butch" Harmon, the son of Claude Harmon Sr., the 1948 Masters champion who was best known for his inventive short game play. Consequently, Tiger is able to hit pitch shots on varying trajectories and with different degrees of spin. This versatility sets him apart from many other players today and allows him to get the ball up and in—from out in the fairway and from around the green.

Frankly, no club golfer, and no other pro golfer except maybe Phil Mickelson, can hit a pitching wedge as far as Tiger. Mickelson, however, is not as accurate as Tiger because he takes an overly long backswing. Tiger's action is more compact, and thus more controlled. Also, because his wrists don't cock dramatically at the top, he's able to delay the hit coming down, generating more power when he needs it.

The typical amateur hits a full pitching wedge only about 80 to 100 yards, the pro around 120 yards. Tiger hits this club 150 yards when swinging full-out. Although average golfers can't match Tiger's distance, you are capable of copying Tiger's two full pitching wedge techniques that are about to be taught to you: one that allows the ball to land softly on the green and release toward the hole and another that allows the ball to spin back toward the hole. It's important to learn these two full wedge shots by reading my analysis of Tiger's techniques and carefully studying photographs and artwork illustrating his pitching actions. Knowing when to play these two shots and how to hit them confidently will allow you to put yourself in the most ideal scoring positions. As Butch Harmon told me: "I can turn seven out of ten ninety shooters into eighty shooters just by teaching them how to pitch."

If you are to become a more complete player, it's also vitally important that you learn Tiger's two unique short wedge play techniques, as well as some innovative trouble play methods, all covered in this chapter.

The Forward-Release Full-Pitch Shot

During a round of golf, you will face several pitch shots to greens that are unguarded by a bunker or water hazard in the front. In cases where the pin is located on the back tier of a two-level green, and there's trouble behind the putting surface, the smart play is to feed the ball to the hole, landing it short of the cup and letting it roll forward, or release, toward the target. This is the highest percentage shot to hit, because usually the worst thing

Before hitting a forward-release pitch, check the distance to your landing target by looking at a yardage book or yardage markers, or by checking with your caddie, as Tiger does with Fluff.

the ball will do is finish a few yards short or long of the hole. Unless you're two or three holes down late in a match, it's pointless to attack the flag and run the risk of overshooting the green.

Preswing Fundamentals. Before setting up to play the shot, it is essential that you stand behind it and pick a specific spot on the green to land the ball on. Since you want to hit a slight draw that lands with overspin, your target should be a small area of green to the right of the flag and short of it. Make sure that you figure out the exact distance to your intended target by talking with your caddie, as Tiger does with his caddie, Mike "Fluff"

Cowan; by using course yardage markers as your reference; or by reading a yardage book. Next, do what Tiger and Jack Nicklaus do so well—let your eyes track the flight of the shot, from the ball to the flagstick. This procedure sends a positive message to your brain, allows you to set up for the shot with a confident total-body attitude, and encourages the correct swinging action. Nicklaus is such a strong believer in the eye-tracking process—what he calls "going to the movies"—that he never sets up to swing until he sees the perfect shot play in his mind. This proven preswing process of Nicklaus's has obviously been adopted by Tiger. He stares so intently at the target that, by the concentrative look in his eyes, you'd swear he was getting ready to recut the Hope diamond. This same mental discipline will allow you to hit more pinpoint pitch shots during a round of golf and save par in the process.

Setup Fundamentals. Aim the pitching wedge's clubface at a small area of green to the right of the flag. This allows for the right-to-left spin that will be imparted on the ball. Set your hands in line with the ball, which ideally should be positioned a few inches ahead of the midpoint of your stance. This relatively forward ball position will encourage the clubhead to sweep fluidly through the fairway grass. Taking a shoulder-width closed stance—with the right foot a few inches farther away from the target line—will allow you to swing the club on a wider arc and further ensure the desired sweeping hit through impact. Incidentally, the target line is an imaginary line running from the ball to the target. This type of pitch shot should not be played out of an open stance, with the ball back and the hands ahead of it. That's because you do not want to swing on a steep plane, hit down on the ball, take a thick divot, and impart backspin on the shot. Again, you want the ball to land short of the target, then release slowly toward the hole.

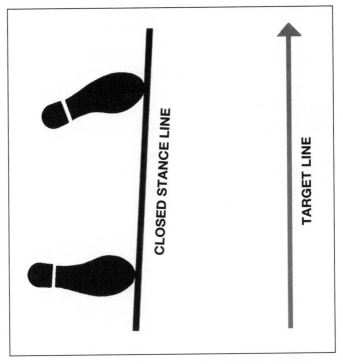

Closing your stance will allow you to swing the club on a flatter plane and hit the ball with a clean sweeping action.

Grip or hold the club lightly, maintaining that same grip pressure throughout the swing; this hold promotes a smoother action and discourages you from pulling the club down hard into the turf.

Two other elements of Tiger's swing will allow you to swing the club on a flatter, or more inside, backswing path, then down on the desired shallow arc. When gripping the pitching wedge, turn your hands away from the target slightly, so the Vs formed by your thumbs and forefingers point up virtually at your right shoulder. This is what's referred to as a strong position, and it's used by some fine wedge players, including John Daly. Daly, known for his amazing power, proved what a great wedge player he is en route to winning the 1995 British Open, played at the Royal and Ancient Golf Club of St. Andrews, in Scotland.

In order to ensure that you make contact with the ball just as the club is moving upward, place 60 percent of your weight on your right foot and tilt your head slightly more to the right.

Backswing Fundamentals. In taking the club back, it's necessary that you control the action by turning your shoulders in a clockwise direction. It's this action that allows you to correctly swing the club inside the target line (inside path) almost automatically. It's also critical that you keep the wrists locked; this will help you swing the club low to the ground during the takeaway. Keeping the club low is vital, since it's this move and this move only that promotes the wide and more powerful backswing arc needed to propel the ball all the way to the hole.

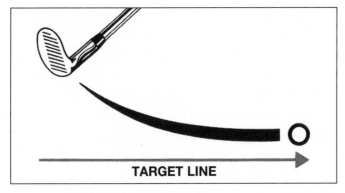

To hit the forward-release pitch correctly, the club must be swung back along an inside path.

Triggering the wide arc is one thing; preserving it via a one-piece takeaway action is another. As you continue swinging the club away, maintain the stiff-wristed position while at the same time extending your arms and club back. According to Don Trahan, one of America's top teachers, the best way to match Tiger's wide width of arc position is to imagine swinging the club into a catcher's mitt about 2 feet behind you and 1 foot above the ground.

The wrists, particularly the right one, should not begin hinging until the hands are level with your chest and well past your body and about 75 percent of your weight has been transferred to your right foot. If you

---

turn correctly, you will feel pressure build in the heel area of your right foot and in your right hip.

It is critical at this point in the swing that you keep your right knee braced. This bracing action is vitally important because it allows you to build resistance between the upper and lower body. It's this resistance that creates torque and, ultimately, allows you to hit the ball as solidly as possible. In order to stay in balance and control the club to the best of your ability, keep your left foot planted on the ground. Encourage a free swing and stronger turning action of the shoulders by allowing your head to rotate slightly, away from the target.

Once the wrists start cocking or hinging, begin turning your hips in a clockwise direction. But don't ever let them rotate too much, or you will swing the club too far inside the target line. This fault causes you to exaggerate the draw-flight and hit the ball so low that it will run through the green. As the hips coil, the arms should swing the club up and back to the three-quarter point, while the shoulders complete their turn. Ideally, in hitting this type of full-pitch shot, the left shoulder should turn under the chin and rotate nearly 90 degrees.

What's unique about Tiger is how the parts of his body slowly gather themselves on the backswing, in one rhythmic coordinated action. There is so much going on during this very intricate backswing, yet because Tiger never rushes the action, and depends on the big muscles of his body for control, it looks simple. In fact, a slow-paced musical piece by Mozart would perfectly accompany this part of his swing. Follow Tiger's example and you'll tie together the movements of the club with those of your body.

Downswing Fundamentals. Because Tiger's full-pitch backswing is shorter and slower than his long swing action, his downswing will not be a reflexive action. Like Nick Price, one of the world's greatest wedge game shot makers, Tiger triggers the downward action by pushing his right hip downward and inward. This one key sets off a chain reaction that allows the entire downswing to operate essentially on automatic pilot. His arms and the club drop down on the desired shallower path while his wrists remain cocked and his right shoulder tilts downward. The combination of these actions poises Tiger to keep his upper body well behind the ball in the impact zone, or hitting area, while sliding his knees gently toward the target.

Tiger's slight knee slide is also a vitally important element of his downswing action, namely because it encourages weight to shift to his front foot and his front hip to start rotating counterclockwise. This clearing action of the hip opens a passageway for the arms and hands to swing the club freely down into the ball, then through it. The added bonus of employing this knee slide is that it allows you to maintain the ideal shallower downswing path and nip the ball cleanly off the fairway grass.

Copying Tiger's knee action will allow you to contact the ball cleanly and crisply.

What's important for you to realize here is that Tiger's lower body plays the lead role on the downswing while the upper body plays the supporting role.

In analyzing Tiger's lower body action, it becomes evident that the clearing action of the left hip is what encourages the forearms to rotate counterclockwise. As a result, the toe of the club leads the heel, causing a slight degree of draw-spin to be imparted on the ball.

In order that the upper body remain passive, Tiger keeps his head behind the ball. The resistance of the head allows Tiger to keep the club on target during the downswing and, ultimately, apply the "sweetspot," or the central area of the clubface, to the ball.

The more vigorously Tiger pushes his right hip downward and inward at the beginning of the downswing, the faster his arms and clubhead move. Nevertheless, his true power key involves his right wrist. Tiger keeps it hinged until the club starts to level out and move from inside to along the target line. You should, too. Commenting on this unique movement, the original guru golf instructor, Phil Ritson of the Orange County National Golf Center in Orlando, Florida, says:

By striving to keep the right wrist flexed back as long as possible through the impact zone, you will be accomplishing something that's very important to making pure contact. It means you are keeping the right hand from prematurely flipping the clubhead off line, and also retaining the clubhead's maximum speed until the last possible instant.

I can't be too emphatic on this point: For any normal full shot, you must not *make any conscious effort to hit or add power to the shot through impact. Any attempt to hit with your hands will only serve to throw away clubhead speed prematurely, as well as increase the chance of delivering the clubhead inaccurately to the ball and mishitting the shot.*

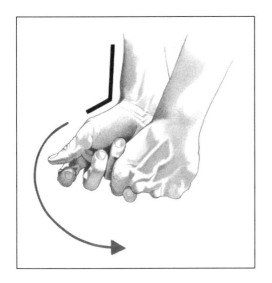

Keeping the right wrist flexed back as long as possible is a vital key to hitting a powerful forward-release pitch shot.

Tiger's follow-through and finish are full because he accelerates the club through the ball at such a high speed. If you tend to slow down in the hitting area and stop at the ball, try visualizing yourself swinging into a full finish position before you even step into the shot. This preswing mental drill will encourage you to hit nicely through the ball, rather than at it.

The Full One-Bounce and Suck-Back Shot

At least once during a round of golf, you will face a full-pitch shot to a green guarded in front by a water hazard or yawning bunker, with the pin cut in its front portion. Obviously, in this situation you could play a shot similar to the one just reviewed. However, in order to hit the shot close to the hole, you would need to land the ball in the fringe nearest you while running the risk of ending up in one or the other of these lurking hazards. If you hit the ball a trifle too easy, you will probably make bogey or worse. If you hit the ball a little hard, you're likely to land in the back portion of the green and, eventually, three-putt. In such a situation, it's better to take the trouble out of play and hit a wedge shot that lands past the hole before sucking back toward it. Tiger makes this happen by imparting a combination of left-to-right cut-spin, and backspin, on the ball. Let me now show you how to work the same kind of short game magic and put yourself in birdie position.

Preswing Fundamentals. As always, see the shot come to life in your mind's eye before you swing. In this situation, you want to hit a shot that fades toward the target, so visualize the ball starting its flight left of the flag, then curving in the air toward it. You also want to make sure you avoid flirting with trouble fronting the green. So stare at the top of the flag, since this visual key will encourage you to hit the ball with enough power to carry the trouble and land beyond the hole. Again, once it lands it will spin back toward the hole.

Setup Fundamentals. Tiger plays the ball back in his stance, with his hands ahead, since this address position promotes an upright backswing and, ultimately, a sharp hit. He aims his feet and body at a point left of target

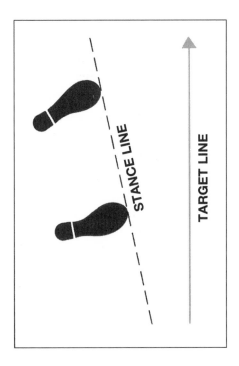

In setting up to play the one-bounce and suck-back shot, be sure to take an open stance.

where he wants the ball to start its flight, and sets the club down dead square to the flagstick. Many fine wedge players, including Tom Kite and Fred Couples, set up the same way Tiger does. That's because this address position encourages you to swing the club back outside the target line, then down into the ball. It's this unique out-to-in swing path that enables you to impart the desired degree of backspin on the ball.

I've also noticed that, in setting up to play this type of left-to-right pitch, Tiger weakens his grip by pointing the Vs of both hands up at his chin. I suggest you grip the club the same way, particularly since this hold further encourages an upright out-to-in swing. Also, grip the handle more firmly with the last three fingers of the left hand. On a scale of 1 to 10 that goes from super-light to superfirm, your grip pressure should be about 7. This hold will allow you to keep the clubface open slightly through impact and to hit the desired high left-to-right shot.

Backswing Fundamentals. Swing the club along the line of your open feet, knees, hips, and shoulders. Because of

To set yourself in position to hit down sharply and impart backspin on the ball, swing the club back on an upright plane.

---

where you positioned the ball, the club will move upward very quickly. Still, as a safeguard against flattening the swing, allow your wrists to hinge sooner than normal.

When Tiger plays this shot, he keeps his head perfectly still, as you should, simply because the steady position will prevent you from swaying and swinging the pitching wedge on an overly wide arc. On this shot, you need to swing the club back up quite quickly, to ensure a narrow backswing arc and encourage a strong descending hit. Stop when you feel yourself reach the three-quarter point of the backswing.

Downswing Fundamentals. Thrust the club downward with your arms and turn your right hand *under* your left. The ball-back position will allow you to contact the ball very solidly at impact, a split second before the clubface squares itself up. As a result, you will impart the desired spin on the ball. If you employ the correct hit-and-hold action, you'll feel some resistance as the club makes solid contact with the ball.

The Short Floater

Some of today's course designers are modeling greens after those of renowned green architects from the past, such as Donald Ross and A. W. Tillinghast. Both of these geniuses were known for creating sloping greens with tiny plateau areas for placing the pin. When the greenkeeper positions the hole on one of these small plateau

Playing the ball back in the stance is one reason why Tiger can trap the ball like this at impact.

areas, it's difficult to hit the ball close unless you play a specialty of Tiger's: a floating shot that lands near the pin and stops dead. Here's how to hit it.

Preswing Fundamentals. In preparing to hit this shot, visualize yourself swinging under the ball, then through it. Next, see the ball floating softly into the air, then landing and stopping close by the cup.

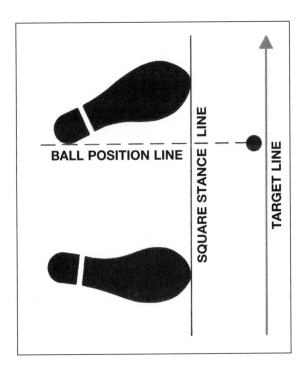

BALL POSITION LINE

SQUARE STANCE LINE

TARGET LINE

You will consistently hit accurate floater shots if you take a square stance.

Setup Fundamentals. Play this shot with a sand wedge. Position the ball opposite your left heel or slightly behind it. In practice, determine which position works best. Set up square, aiming your feet and body parallel to the target line. Set the club square to the target. Grip lightly to promote a tension-free swing.

Backswing Fundamentals. Swing the club back to the halfway point like Tiger, allowing your left wrist to bend inward, or "cup," in a slightly concave position. Many top players advocate a flat left wrist position because it indicates that the clubface is also square in relation to the swing's arc. All the same, you want the clubface to open wide going back, and a cupped left wrist position promotes this ideal clubface position—in fact, to such a degree that the sand wedge's normal 55 degrees of loft will increase to about 70 degrees. Cupping the left wrist also makes it virtually impossible for you to close the clubface at impact and hit a low running shot. Knowing this before you swing will heighten your confidence.

In playing the short floater, be sure to cup your left wrist on the backswing.

I also suggest that, like Tiger, you allow the right wrist to hinge. Not only does this free-hinging action enhance your feel for the clubhead, but it also allows you to pace the swing perfectly and hit the shot the correct distance.

Downswing Fundamentals. Think of nothing except briskly rotating your hips counterclockwise while maintaining the same cupped and hinged positions of the wrists. Preserving these wrist positions in the hitting area is what allows you to maintain the loft of the club through impact. This is Tiger's secret to hitting short on-target wedge shots to the tightest pins, set on plateau areas of the greens.

Keep rotating your hips through impact to accelerate the club under the ball. The faster you rotate the hips, the higher and farther the ball will fly.

The Short Pitch-and-Run Shot

One of the toughest course situations to face is a 40-to-60-yard shot off tightly mowed fairway grass, especially if the pin is positioned on the bottom portion of a firm green. Even when there is no trap guarding the front entranceway to the green, this shot can be very intimidating to average golfers fearful of hitting the ball thin with the sand wedge.

Frankly, even PGA Tour pros find it difficult to loft the ball into the air off a very tight lie. That's pre-

Rotating your hips counterclockwise, through impact, is vitally important when playing a short floating shot.

cisely why the smartest players, such as Tiger, take a pitching wedge out of their bags, instead of a sand wedge or 60-degree wedge, and play a pitch-and-run shot. In this situation, the running shot is far easier to play, particularly if there is a strong wind at your back. Additionally, it's the percentage play simply because you don't need to swing back as far or accelerate the club quite as hard as you do when hitting a lofted shot with one of the other two wedges.

World-renowned teacher David Leadbetter, of Lake Nona Golf Club in Orlando, Florida, obviously agrees with Tiger's strategy. His general philosophy is that when there's only flat ground between the ball and the hole, a pitch-and-run shot is ideal.

This is definitely a shot you should learn, particularly if you're planning a golf vacation to Ireland or Scotland, where you will surely run into similar situations on their wonderful links courses by the sea.

Preswing Fundamentals. You want to land the ball short of the green so that it bounces a couple of times before rolling to the hole. How close you land the ball to the green depends on the strength of the wind and the hardness of the fairways. The firmness of the green itself should also be taken into consideration. Obviously, if the wind is blowing hard and the fairway and green are both baked hard by the sun, you want to allow for more roll. Figure on landing the ball around 15 yards from the green's front edge. Normally, however, you should focus on a landing spot that is about 10 yards from the green. Before taking your setup, actually see the shot come to life in your mind's eye: Watch the ball hit the fairway, bounce into the air, then roll over the fairway grass, through the fringe, and finally onto the green.

Setup Fundamentals. Tiger plays this shot out of either a slightly closed or square stance, with the ball positioned midway between his feet or a little ahead of that point. Tiger doesn't lock himself into one setup position. I assume that's because, like Seve Ballesteros, he realizes that as human beings we are constantly subject to change.

In 1987, while collaborating on the book *Natural Golf*, Ballesteros told me that on mornings when his body feels a little stiff, he'll play the ball farther forward in his stance to allow the clubface more time to return to a square position at impact. On days when his body feels nice and loose and his swing is naturally faster, he adjusts by playing the ball farther back in his stance. This change allows him to stay behind the ball through impact and hit a crisp, on-target shot.

I suggest you experiment to see which ball position and stance works best. I would never recommend, however, that you assume an open stance and play the ball behind the midpoint of your stance. The reason is that your backswing will tend to steepen, and as a result you will hit too sharply down on the ball and hit the wrong type of shot. This is a shot that should fly fairly low and run along the ground. Don't let your stance get too narrow, either, since that will also cause your swing to steepen. Instead, spread your feet apart only slightly less than shoulder width to promote a wider swing arc.

Grip the club more firmly, with the last three fingers of your left hand and middle two fingers of your right hand, to encourage your arms and shoulders to control the swinging action of the club, on the way back and on the way down. An overly loose hold on the club will cause you to break your wrists prematurely and hit anything but the intended shot.

Just before you swing, make sure that your hands are a couple of inches ahead of the ball.

Backswing Fundamentals. Swing the club back inside the target line, while keeping your wrists locked and

When hitting the short pitch and run, be sure to release your right hand freely over your left through impact.

lower body fairly quiet. To help you swing the club along the correct path, to waist level, concentrate on turning your shoulders gently in a clockwise direction.

Downswing Fundamentals. Swing the club through, again to waist level, with your right hand releasing, or rotating, freely over your left. The proper feeling on the downswing should be one of brushing the clubhead through the sparse grass. Working your knees toward the target will help you employ the correct action, plus swing more rhythmically.

How to Hit a Short Pitch Shot from Heavy Rough

To hit a strong pitch from heavy rough, hold on to the club more tightly with your left hand and accelerate your arms into the follow-through.

Play the ball back in an exaggerated open stance—that is, with your left foot several inches farther away from the target line than your right foot. Set the clubface in a square position, or perpendicular to your target.

Swing the club back on a very steep angle, or plane, allowing your wrists to cock early in the takeaway.

The heavy grass can twist the club into a closed impact position very easily, so hold on more tightly with your left hand to help you keep the clubface square. Pull the club down to a spot just behind the ball, then swing fluidly into the follow-through position as Tiger does in the accompanying photo. If you accelerate your arms and the club powerfully, the ball will pop up into the air and fly toward the target.

The Secrets to Hitting a Blind Pitch Stiff to the Hole

Many golfers panic when they face a pitch shot to an elevated green, with no flag visible. They feel disoriented simply because they don't take the time to walk up the hill and see where the flag is positioned. As a result, they tend to look up, or peek, before impact, causing the shot to be mishit. Don't make the same mistake.

Logically, what you need to get right in this situation, before you actually swing, is direction. So, after you walk up to the green and see where the flagstick is positioned, pick a tall tree behind the green as your aiming point. That way, when you stand over the ball, unable to see the flag, you'll know exactly where to aim. Being sure about where to aim relaxes you and makes you confident. Those are two ingredients for making a smooth swing and producing good shots.

In setting up, take one more club—for example, a pitching wedge instead of a sand wedge—to allow for the uphill shot. Next, pick out a precise area on the back of the ball to focus your eyes on.

Make your normal backswing.

Coming through, try to watch the club hit the ball.

How to Handle Clover

It is not uncommon to face a shot out of clover, particularly when playing a course in the northeastern United States, such as Winged Foot, where Tiger competed in the 1997 PGA Championship. Clover looks innocent, but it can be very troublesome if you don't know what to do.

When facing a short pitching wedge shot out of clover, use your sand wedge instead. That's because the leaves are likely to get stuck between the ball and the clubface at impact and cause the ball to fly farther than normal.

In this situation, you don't want to employ a one-piece takeaway or the club will get stuck in the clover for a split second, throwing it off its natural inside path. Instead, allow your wrists to hinge early in the takeaway and swing the club up steeply to the three-quarter point.

Make your normal downswing action, but keep your head behind the ball longer to promote a higher, quick-stopping shot.

What to Do When Pitching off Wet Fairways

Sometimes you will find your ball lying on a wet fairway, with such limited water on the grass that you are not entitled to a drop under the casual water rule. In hitting a shot off wet grass, make a more rounded swing and sweep the ball. Don't hit down or you'll take too deep a divot and mishit the shot.

Playing the ball opposite your left heel and swinging more slowly are intelligent strategies, since they both encourage a more sweeping hit. Remember, in losing clubhead speed you will lose distance. So, if you face a shot with a sand wedge, play the pitching wedge instead.

How to Handle a Downhill Lie off Fairway Grass

When facing a pitching wedge shot off the fairway, play a sand wedge to allow for the club's effective loft being reduced at impact.

In setting up, play the ball back in your stance, so your hands are naturally positioned ahead of it. Tilt your body perpendicular to the slope so that, in effect, you give yourself a flat lie. It's also critical that you place slightly more weight on your right foot and keep it there throughout the entire action, to prevent yourself from losing your balance and falling forward.

Make your normal backswing, but concentrate on emphasizing arm and wrist action over body turn, since this will further help you maintain your balance and stay in control of the club. Keeping your head steady is also paramount to making a balanced on-plane swing.

Maintain the flex in your knees at the start of the downswing (don't straighten up), then let the clubhead follow the ball down the slope through impact. Because the upper body tends to slide past the ball, the releasing action of the club will be hindered. The clubface will stay open slightly at impact, causing the ball to fade slightly. Allow for this by aiming left of the target; the steeper the slope, the more you should aim left.

How to Handle an Uphill Lie off Fairway Grass

If you face a sand wedge shot off a severe uphill lie, take a pitching wedge, since the effective loft of the club will increase at impact.

When setting up, tilt your body to the right so that you again effectively give yourself a flat lie. Aim your body and club a little bit to the right of the target, because the tendency is to hit a pull shot left of the target.

Protect yourself against swaying on the backswing by keeping your left foot planted on the ground. Also, minimize your body action and accentuate your arm-swing so that you prevent yourself from falling back onto your right foot during the downswing and hitting a slice.

In swinging down, keep your head behind the ball and accelerate the club through the impact zone, following the natural slope of the terrain.

What to Do When the Ball Is Above Your Feet

More and more architects are designing courses with rolling fairways, trying to bring a feel of the British links courses to America. That's why smart players prepare themselves for any lie.

When the ball is above your feet, aim your body and the clubface of your pitching wedge square to a point right of the target to allow for the draw-flight that you will automatically produce owing to the sideslope. The steeper the slope, the more you should aim to the right.

Once you set up, make your normal swing.

What to Do When the Ball Is Below Your Feet

When the ball is on a slope below your feet, toe the clubface in slightly.

Aim your body and club to the left of the target, to allow for the fade shot you will hit off this lie. The steeper the slope, the more you should aim to the left. Once you are in a comfortable and correct setup position, make your normal pitching swing.

How to Deal with a Depression

Even the flattest-looking fairways, like those on many old Florida courses, have slight depressions in the grass. When your ball lands in one of these dips, you can't just aim straight at the flag and make your normal inside-square-inside swing or you will probably hit a thin shot over the green.

From such a lie, the best strategy is to take an open stance, swing the club back outside the target line, then swing across it coming through to avoid the protruding area of ground behind the ball. You'll hit a solid shot, but the ball will fade, so allow for this flight when aiming.

How to Hit a Knockdown Wedge into a Strong Wind

Hitting a low shot that cheats the wind and lands with a whole lot of backspin is a skill Tiger has down pat. Here's how to do it:

Set up with your feet parallel to the target line. Play the ball a few inches back in this square stance, so your hands are positioned well ahead of the ball. Place about 60 percent of your weight on your left foot.

Extend the club back very low in the takeaway, and well inside the target line, while keeping your head perfectly still. Continue swinging the club back to the three-quarter point, on a flat path.

Let your hands lead the downswing, with the club staying low to the ground through impact. Keep the follow-through action short, since what you're trying to do here is hit sort of a low-flying punch shot.

How to Escape from the Trees

Before playing safe out of trees, look up for a better escape route.

Very often a golfer who lands in the trees looks over the situation quickly, then pitches out sideways to the fairway. Tiger, on the other hand, looks for portholes in the trees, spaces of air that he can launch a ball into and through.

The advantage of playing any one of the three wedges is that they all get the ball up quickly. Still, encourage a higher shot by playing the ball well forward of the stance's midpoint and keeping your upper body weight back on your right side through impact. Also, release your right hand under your left, since this allows you to increase the effective loft of the club and scoop the ball high into the air.

What to Do When the Ball Is at the Base of a Grassy Bank

Pretend you just hit a ball over a green, down a grassy bank behind it. The lie is tight and the pin is positioned on the top tier of the green closest to you. In this situation, instead of trying to hit a lofted shot, borrow a shot from Tiger's bag—the "bank" shot. Provided the wall of grass in front of you is not very steep, simply bump the ball into the bank so that it bounces up onto the green and trickles to the hole.

Using a pitching wedge, play the ball in the middle of your stance. Swing the club back inside the target line, controlling the action with your hands and arms. Don't exaggerate body action. Coming down, keep your wrists locked and keep the club moving low through impact.

Feel as if you are "raking" the ball toward the target through impact.

What to Do When the Ball Lies in Water by the Green

If at least one half of the ball is above the surface of the water, it's worth playing the shot.

Don't take a drop and incur a penalty stroke if half the ball is above the water's surface and, ideally, you can stand with at least one foot on land.

To recover, play the ball back in an open stance, open the face of a sand wedge, swing on a steep plane, and contact a spot just behind the ball, as you would when recovering from a greenside bunker.

Pitching Magic

How to Play Out of Sandy Rough

You don't need to be playing the links courses of the British Isles to face this kind of shot; you'll run into this lie in America, particularly on the oceanside courses of South Carolina or the coastline courses on the eastern end of Long Island, New York.

The natural inclination is to hit down sharply from such a lie, when in fact a sweeping swing works better. Hitting down is a mistake because the club tends to dig too deeply into the sandy turf. As a result, you only advance the ball a few yards.

When looking for distance, take a closed stance, swing the club back on a flatter plane than normal, and keep the club moving low through impact.

How to Recover from Hardpan

When confronting this greenside hardpan lie, reach for a 60-degree wedge.

To play an extrashort shot from trodden turf or a dry hard spot, select a 60-degree wedge. Take a square or a slightly open stance, with the ball positioned a few inches behind your left heel and the clubface square to your target. Keep your hands ahead of the ball at address and in the hitting area. Your wrists should also stay locked as you accelerate the club into impact and contact the ball sharply on the descent.

PITCHING DRILLS

DRILL #1 (To Acquaint Yourself with the Feeling of Sweeping the Club Through the Ball)

The essence of the forward-release pitching technique is swinging the club low through impact so it makes clean contact with the ball. To get a feel for the proper sweeping action, practice hitting shots off a piece of old carpet. Lightly brush the carpet with the sole of the club as you swing through the ball. Use that same type of action when hitting off fairway grass.

DRILL #2 (For Learning to Hit Down Sharply)

Some golfers, particularly women, just can't get themselves to hit down sharply at impact. However, you need to employ this action to hit the one-bounce and suckback pitch shot from the fairway.

To train yourself to hit down on the ball, practice hitting shots out of bad lies in the rough. Playing the ball back in an open stance will allow you to swing the club on the correct steep plane.

DRILL #3 (For Improving Touch)

To enhance your feel for guiding the clubhead back to the ball at impact with your left hand, practice hitting short wedge shots with your left hand only. Grip more firmly if you have great difficulty returning the clubface squarely to the ball.

DRILL #4 (For Learning Distance Control)

Since for most people their right hand is the strongest, it is the one they use to put oomph behind the shot. To help you learn how to control distance, practice hitting shots with your right hand only, each time varying the speed of your swing slightly.

After finishing this drill, put both hands on the club and hit shots to targets set out at different distances.

DRILL #5 (For Learning New Shots)

The best way to learn new shots is to go out on the course, in the quiet of a morning or late afternoon, and practice hitting shots out of all kinds of lies. Be imaginative. Put one ball down in the deep grass, another on the side of a hill, another half in sand and half in grass, and so forth. Try to recover using a variety of clubs and a variety of techniques. At the end of the session, you'll be surprised how much you learn about what you can and cannot do with a club.

DRILL #6 (For Learning How to Loft the Ball High into the Air)

While attending Stanford University, Tiger used to practice hitting pitch shots over the dorms. You don't have to take such extreme measures to learn to hit high wedge shots.

Practice hitting golf balls over a badminton net in your backyard. Having a net to hit over will encourage you to open the clubface more at address, keep your head behind the ball on the downswing, and accelerate the club under and through the ball.

DRILL #7 (For Learning How to Handle a Pressure Situation)

When practicing short pitches, pretend that you have to hit the ball a certain distance from the hole to win an imaginary match. Keep moving your target spot closer to the hole so you get used to pressure situations. Also, make things tougher and more interesting by changing the lie of the ball from time to time.

DRILL #8 (For Learning How to Swing Smoothly)

If you tend to top short pitch shots, it could be that you're swinging too fast. This fault usually causes you to lift up through impact, with the sole of the club hitting the top of the ball.

To smooth out a fast tempo, simply count "one" as you swing back, "two" as you swing down and through the shot.

DRILL #9 (For Fixing Your Setup)

If you tend to push short pitches off to the right, you could be playing the ball too far forward in your stance and aligning your body well right of target. If you tend to pull pitches left of target and take deep divots, you could be playing the ball too far back in your stance and exaggerating your open alignment.

To check your alignment and ball position, have your local pro or a friend videotape you. Next, adjust your setup accordingly. Depending on the type of pitch shot you're hitting, it's okay to assume a slightly open or closed stance. Just don't exaggerate these unique setup positions.

CHIPPING MAGIC

Reading the lie correctly, knowing when to give the ball more air time than ground time— or vice versa—and alternating between a wristless and a wristy stroke are Tiger's vital strategies for hitting the ball close to the cup.

Many amateur golfers are under the naive impression that professional players hit every green in regulation. If you share that view, listen up. As well as Tiger and other world-class professionals play, they hit only an average of twelve greens per round. What you can conclude from this statistic is that even the best players in the world don't hit every iron shot at their intended target. Consequently, to save par on the other six holes, they have to hit some kind of greenside shot, usually a chip, within one-putt range. They succeed most of the time, but few are as creative around the greens as Tiger.

Conversely, club-level players waste strokes around the green. The typical high-handicapper often hits chips well past the hole, or a few yards short of it, and takes three strokes to get down. Considering they probably miss around twelve greens per round, that's a lot of wasted strokes.

One fault the high handicap player makes is using only one favorite club, usually a seven iron, to hit all types of chip shots. Frankly, this makes about as much sense as a hunter trying to use the same gun to kill a rabbit and a bear. If you limit yourself to one club, particularly one that's not nearly as lofted as any of your wedges, you are not giving yourself a fair chance to chip the ball close to the cup. The lie of the ball, the distance to a landing spot, the texture and topography of the land between the ball and the hole, and the speed of the green vary greatly. More important, they are variables that must be considered every single time you face a chip shot. Therefore, even if you are blessed with exceptional eye-hand coordination and have a superb feel for distance, you are not going to be able to get the job done with just one club.

The main reason that Tiger is such a fine chipper is that he learned to develop numerous chip shots by practicing creatively with a variety of clubs. What he didn't learn that way, Butch Harmon taught him. Tiger has hit so many shots that he can look at a lie and determine quickly what club and what chipping technique will work best. Moreover, he takes the time to rehearse the shot physically, by swinging his arms and hands without holding a club. This immediately gives him a feel for the correct action and tells him how hard to swing. Tiger

In supervising Tiger's practice sessions, Butch Harmon sometimes teaches him new chip shots.

also takes great care to trace the line and the ball's flight by running his eyes along the target line a few times and seeing the shot happen in his mind. All great players do this, but if you watch Tiger in action, whether live at a tournament or on television, you can see that the wheels are really turning inside his head.

Because Tiger is such a precise chipper, holing out so many shots, I know that he has learned the ratios of how long the ball flies in the air and rolls after landing. In hitting the standard sand wedge chip, for example, he plans on the ball having 75 percent air time, 25 percent

---

Chipping Magic   61

roll time. On the other extreme is the four iron, with only 10 percent air time, 90 percent roll time. In between are the eight iron at a ratio of 40 to 60 percent air time to roll time, the nine iron at 50-50, and the pitching wedge at 60-40. Included in Tiger's repertoire is one other popular chipping club—the three wood, which he uses to hit a unique shot Butch Harmon taught him (see color insert).

Although Tiger uses a variety of clubs to chip with, the most popular club in his bag is the sand wedge, a club he often uses to play lofted or running chip shots. Just by making small adjustments in his ball and hand positions at address, and tiny changes in his swing, he is able to chip the ball close to the hole with this club.

In contrast, many average golfers never think about using the sand wedge. They think it is only to be used in bunkers. Not true. If you have limited time to practice, it pays to get to know this club well, simply because it enables you to hit a wide variety of shots in a far-ranging number of course situations.

Many of you will find it easier to chip with a sand wedge, simply because it's shorter and more lofted than the other irons. What's more, it's easier to hit out of bad lies with this club. Even more important, you can be a little off in your execution and still land the ball on the green. That's not the case with other clubs. For example, in chipping with a seven iron, if you swing a little too hard, you can send the ball flying over the green. Because the sand wedge has so much loft built into the clubface, it allows you to play aggressive chips with no worry about hitting the ball over the green.

As much as Tiger likes chipping with a sand wedge, he chooses the club that will loft the ball to his preselected landing spot, then roll it the rest of the way to the hole. When using a low-lofted club, such as a four iron, his stroke is shorter and slower. When using a more lofted club, the opposite is true. Generally, too, the closer the ball is to the hole the more lofted the club he uses.

Most often, Tiger prefers to use a wristless, pendulum-type chipping stroke, as this method tends to stand up better under pressure. That's because the big muscles of the arms and shoulders control the action, rather than the hands and wrists. This type of action produces a low running chip shot.

In cases when the ball is sitting down slightly, Tiger incorporates some hand and wrist action into his swing and steepens his action slightly to pop the ball out of the bad lie or heavier grass. The shot he produces flies higher in the air and stops more quickly.

To shoot the lowest possible score that you are capable of shooting and to lower your handicap in the process, you must be able to deaden your hands and wrists and play the low, long running chip or liven up your hand-wrist action and hit a high, short pop shot that lands softly and rolls quietly a little way to the hole. I will now review these two basic techniques before going into some more sophisticated chip shots and drills for helping you become an expert chipper like Tiger.

The Running Chip

Even before reaching the ball, Tiger begins looking at the general flow of the land to get an idea of the breaks in the green. He goes through this analysis process because he realizes that from a distance the tilt in the terrain is often more obvious. In fact, sometimes when one is standing on the green it can appear flat, even though it has subtle undulations.

Tiger reads chips as seriously as he reads putts.

Once at his ball, Tiger takes a closer look at the slopes, then determines the condition of the grass to get a feel for the speed of the putting surface. Tiger travels the world to compete, so he's very aware that greens vary from country club to country club, just as they do from one of your local courses to the next. Different courses use different grasses. Further, the ball breaks more on fast greens because the ball has to be hit more lightly. When hitting to damp greens or Bermuda grass putting surfaces that are much more coarse in texture than bent grass greens, you must allow for less break due to a slower rolling ball.

Next, Tiger picks a spot to land the ball on. To enhance his feel for playing the chips, Tiger almost always removes his glove.

To help him pick the right club, he rehearses the shot by swinging his hands and arms to and fro, mimicking the motion he will use. After picking what he thinks is the best club, he sees the ball landing on his target spot and rolling to the hole like a putt.

In setting up, Tiger assumes a square, very narrow to slightly open stance, and positions the club square to the ball and perpendicular to his aiming spot. When one is hitting to a level green, this spot is directly in line with the hole. If there are slopes in the putting surface, this spot will be to one side of the hole, depending on whether the slope will turn the ball to the left or right.

Because he wants the club to move on a flat-bottomed arc, Tiger plays the ball only a couple of inches behind his left heel. Amateurs, on the whole,

When setting up for a running chip, it's essential that the club's leading edge be dead square to the ball.

make the mistake of playing the ball off their right heel, which causes them to swing the club on a steep plane and hit fat chip shots.

To further encourage a level pendulum action, Tiger usually sets his hands in line with the ball, just as he does when putting. Additionally, he snuggles up close to the ball, with his eyes directly over it.

Although Tiger normally uses an interlock grip to play chips, he sometimes drapes his left forefinger over the first three fingers of his right hand for added control on tricky shots. This innovative chipping grip gives him greater security, further preventing the wrists from hinging. You may want to try this unique chipping grip to determine whether it works well for you. Whatever grip you choose to play with, grip more firmly than lightly, as this will help you keep the club square to your target throughout the stroke. Also, grip down on the club slightly as Tiger, Greg Norman, Ray Floyd, Gary Player, and other expert chippers do. Why? Your hands are the only connection to the club, so by bringing them closer to the clubhead you enhance your feel for making the right length stroke for the shot at hand. "You get the feeling that you're tossing the ball to the hole, so controlling distance is far easier," Norman told me while collaborating with me a few years ago on an instructional cover story for *GOLF Magazine.*

On the backswing, Tiger keeps his head, knees, and wrists quiet. Only his arms and shoulders are used to swing the club virtually straight back along the target line. On longer chips the club swings a little bit inside the line, due to the added clockwise rotation of the shoulders. Keeping the wrists quiet allows Tiger to swing the club back low to the ground. When you take the club back in this fashion you give yourself the best chance of returning it low to the ground and sweeping the ball cleanly off the turf.

On the downswing, Tiger always maintains his steady body position. Only when using a short iron does he turn his right hip and knee toward the target. That's because the added loft built into these clubs allows him to be more aggressive. Normally, he lets only his arms and shoulders return the club to the ball, then through it. The feeling you should get when swinging the club through impact is one of brushing the grass. There should be no sense of hitting down. In fact, according to Gary Smith, a regular analyst for The Golf Channel and

Forming a vivid mental picture of Tiger's backswing action before you swing will help you hit a good running chip.

one of *GOLF Magazine*'s top 100 teachers in America, this shot should be played using a level putting-type stroke. Smith recommends that you stand close to the ball, use a reverse overlap grip, and control the movement of the club with the arms and shoulders. He also believes it's best to keep the same angle of your right wrist throughout the entire action. By keeping your hands and wrists from manipulating the club, you'll prevent mishit shots and run the ball at the target just like Tiger does.

It's no coincidence that Tiger's chip-shot follow-through looks like his putting follow-through. The reason: The strokes are virtually identical.

This stroke of Tiger's may seem robotic, but it has several advantages. Ken Venturi, one of the game's all-time best chippers, whom I worked with on numerous instruction articles for *GOLF Magazine,* is such a supporter of the stiff-wristed stroke that he advises his students to "pretend your wrists are in plaster casts." Venturi told me that this stroke stands up better under pressure because it is controlled by the body's big muscles. Further, he said that keeping the wrists locked encourages you to swing the club on a flat-bottomed arc and sweep the ball cleanly off the grass. (When you exaggerate the hinging action of the wrists on the backswing, you're likely to pick up the club quickly, chop down on the ball or into the turf behind it, and mishit the shot.)

The Lofted Chip

What you want to do here is set yourself up to hit the ball slightly on the descent, since that is the action that will pop the ball softly into the air, over the fringe, then onto the green. Tiger encourages an upright backswing and the right type of hit by playing the ball back in a narrow open stance, with his hands slightly ahead of it. "The open stance also provides you with a better view of the target and, for that reason, encourages you to make an uninhibited tension-free stroke," says Gerald McCullagh, a world-renowned teacher who is based at the Rush Creek Golf Academy in Maple Grove, Minnesota. Adds McCullagh: "Being visually sure of your target before you swing also makes you less apt to lift up your head before impact and mishit the shot."

Tiger also places about 55 percent of his weight on his left foot, leaving it there throughout the stroke to encourage an upright plane of swing and a sharper hit. When he takes his stance his right foot is perpendicular to the target line, since this helps him keep the club in front of his body and swing on an upright plane. Follow Tiger's example; otherwise you are likely to swing the club too far inside the target line and hit a low, fast-running "hot" chip.

When playing the lofted chip, hold the club with a weak grip.

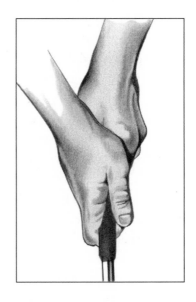

In holding the club, Tiger rotates his right hand more on top of the club, or toward the target, just like Corey Pavin, who is a master of the lofted chip. This weak grip allows you to maintain an open clubface position through impact and loft the ball softly into the air so that it stops quickly next to the hole. Tiger also interlocks his left forefinger and right pinkie. This "interlock" grip allows him to work his hands and wrists more freely. The lofted chip is a far less mechanical shot than the previous running chip. It also requires more finesse, so lighten your grip pressure to enhance your feel for the clubhead.

When you swing the club back, let your wrists hinge slightly in the takeaway, since this promotes an upright plane. Additionally, let your shoulders rock rather than turn. The left shoulder should tilt downward just slightly, rather than turning well around in a clockwise direction, while the right shoulder moves upward. This action is paramount because it forces the club to swing up quite quickly, rather than hugging the ground and swinging inside the ball-hole line. If anything, the club moves a little outside the target line, which is good because this path sets you in position to cut across the ball and produce a shot with added sidespin. This is particularly useful on fast greens when you need to slow the ball down for added control. The shoulder tilt allows the face of the club to shut or point toward the ground on the backswing. This means that, at impact, the club will finish in a slightly open position, lofting the ball over the fringe.

Keep your lower body fairly still on the downswing, but allow your right shoulder to tilt downward slightly while your left tilts upward. This seesaw action (combined with the unhinging of your wrists) allows you to nip the ball off the grass. It's especially helpful when you're hitting off a tight lie or out of a slight depression with a wedge.

Because Tiger hits down on the ball, his followthrough action is short. The resulting shot flies over the fringe grass, then bounces a couple of times before rolling slowly to the hole. The ball will fly higher and stop more quickly on wedge shots, so plan for this.

The seesaw action of Tiger's shoulders helps him lift the ball into the air.

TROUBLE SHOTS: HOW TO RECOVER LIKE TIGER

How to Handle Dirt

The ball is 5 yards off the green but lying on a soft patch of dirt. There's only 10 feet of green between the manicured fringe and the hole. In this situation, you shouldn't play a running chip because all but the fringe grass between the ball and the green is thick.

To avoid mishitting the shot, allow your hands and wrists to work very freely, even more than when playing Tiger's lofted chip shot, explained earlier.

Concentrating on taking a divot, when playing a shot off a dirt patch, will help you accelerate the club through the ball.

Play the ball in the middle of your stance, with your hands behind the ball slightly. Lay the clubface of your sand wedge wide open. Make a short steep backswing, allowing your wrists to hinge early in the takeaway. Swing the club sharply down, contacting a spot about 2 inches behind the ball. The ball will pop up, fly the distance to the hole, and practically stop dead.

What to Do When Blocked by a Bunker

Your ball is to the side of a green, behind a bunker with a very low lip. The ball is sitting on firm turf, and the pin is cut very close to the fringe. You realize that, from this lie, it will be hard to stop the ball close to the hole. Besides, if you used a wedge, you'd probably skull the ball over the green.

You want to play a creative chip shot that runs the ball through the trap. More important, you want the ball to reach the green with just enough speed to roll within easy one-putt range. The seven iron is the perfect club for the job.

Play the ball back in your stance with your hands well ahead. Make a smooth takeaway, letting your arms control the action. Keep your wrists locked and drag the club back very low along the target line. Lead the club into impact, then through the ball with your hands; this allows you to hood the clubface and hit a nice, low running shot through the sand and fringe grass.

What to Do When the Ball Is Half Buried in Bermuda Grass

The ball is sitting down, half buried in thick Bermuda fringe grass. The pin is about 30 feet from you. You're fearful that if you take a sand wedge and hit down sharply into the grass you'll hit the ball fat. Here's the smart play:

Play the ball just behind your left heel with your hands even with it. Line up the club's leading edge with the back center portion of the ball. Balance your weight evenly on the balls of your feet. Using a sand wedge, make a short backswing, controlling the action with your arms and shoulders. Swing the club through in the same way, letting the club contact the top half of the ball. Hitting the shot this way will impart sufficient overspin on the ball, making it pop up out of the grass, then run over the heavy fringe all the way to the hole.

What to Do When You Can't Take Your Normal Stance

The ball is so close to a tree located 15 yards to the side of the green that you can't take your normal setup and hit the ball right-handed as you would normally.

To recover, turn the head of a six iron upside down, so that the toe touches the ground, and set up to play a left-handed shot. Close your stance to encourage a flatter swing. Choke down on the club about an inch and grip firmly to enhance your control.

Make a very compact backswing, keeping your right arm extended and wrists locked. Trigger the downswing by rotating your left hip and knee toward the target. This active motion will allow you to accelerate the club through the ball and contact it more solidly. The shot you produce will rise into the air, land short of the green, then bounce up onto it.

How to Handle Light Rough and a Sloping Green

Your ball lands on a bank behind the green, in light rough. There are only 25 feet of fringe and green between the ball and the hole. Worse still, the green slopes away from you slightly.

Play the ball off your left heel to program loft into the shot. Bend more from the knees than normal to help you stay balanced and make an all-arms swing. Lay the face of your 60-degree wedge wide open so it faces the sky. Grip the club very lightly, because "soft" hands are needed to drop it down gently into the grass behind the ball.

Make a compact backswing, swinging the club straight back with your arms.

Keep your head behind the ball on the way down, as this will allow you to scoop the ball cleanly off the grass. To further help you guide the clubface under the ball and hit a high, soft-landing shot, accelerate your arms and maintain the flex in your knees.

To hit a soft shot off a grassy bank, it's vital that you maintain a deep knee flex on the downswing. The reason: The slightest movement upward can cause you to top the ball.

How to Hit the Sand Cheater

You face a 30-yard shot out of a low-lipped, greenside bunker. This shot is tough enough on its own, but add a water hazard behind the green and you're shaking over the ball. Have no fear—you need not play a sand wedge shot. Hit a long chip with an eight iron, since it is a far easier shot to play.

Play the ball just ahead of the center of a relatively wide square stance. Let your arms hang down naturally and relax them, as you would when putting. As you're holding the club, the Vs formed by your thumbs and forefingers should point midway between your chin and right shoulder, in a "neutral" position. You don't want to hold the club with a weak grip, since this will encourage an exaggerated out-to-in swing. An overly strong grip will promote an exaggerated flat swing. The correct hold will promote a virtually straight-back straight-through stroke.

Make believe that your hands, arms, and shoulders are a triangle cemented together. Now, swing the club back in one piece using that triangle. The wrists should stay locked while you swing the club a couple of feet past your right foot, and up only slightly.

Swing the triangle in the other direction so that the club meets the ball squarely at impact, sending the ball over the low lip toward the hole.

What to Do When the Ball Lies in Wiry Grass

The ball is in wiry greenside grass. Worse still, you only have 5 yards of green between the edge of the manicured fringe and the hole. What do you do?

Start with the ball in the center of a narrow, open stance and also aim your knees, hips, and shoulders left of the target. Weaken your grip, so that the Vs formed by your thumbs and forefingers point up at your chin. This setup position will promote an out-to-in swing path. Hold the clubhead above the ground behind the ball so that you're poised to avoid snagging the club in the grass on the backswing. You'll want to contact the grass with the bounce of the club to loft the ball high into the air. Putting 55 percent of your weight on your right foot and leaving it there throughout the swing will help you accomplish that goal.

Make a wristy backswing and bring the club well outside the target line.

Pull down hard with both hands so that the club makes contact with the grass about 2 inches behind the ball. The ball will fly higher, land softly, then trickle to the hole.

To recover from wiry greenside grass, pull the club down into a spot about 2 inches behind the ball.

THE SHORT FLOATING PITCH

When Tiger hits a high, soft-landing shot from around the green, he increases the flex in his right knee and tilts his right shoulder downward more than normally. These two simple downswing keys, illustrated in the photograph above, allow you to accelerate the club under and through the ball. Notice here that Tiger also plays this shot from a very narrow open stance. That tells you that he's looking to impart added cutspin on the ball, by swinging on a slight out-to-in path.

THE SHORT PITCH-AND-RUN

One chief reason why Tiger is so good at hitting this shot is that he keeps the club moving low through impact. Here you can clearly see the sole of the clubhead actually brushing the ground after the ball was struck. Holding the club more firmly and controlling the swing mainly with your arms and shoulders will help you hit low-flying pitches that run nicely to the hole.

THE LONG POWER-PITCH FROM LONG SCOTTISH GRASS

You can see from the big cut Tiger takes that advancing the ball out of heavy rough requires added clubhead speed. You can generate more power by pulling the club down sharply with your hands and arms. Be sure to hold on tightly to the club so that its face doesn't shut at impact, due to grass grabbing and twisting the hosel.

Tiger played this shot at Troon, in Scotland, when competing in the 1997 British Open. If you are planning to go to Scotland soon, don't leave home without it.

THE SHORT DOWNHILL PITCH FROM ROUGH

Open the clubface of your 60-degree wedge, slightly less if there is a cushion of rough grass under the ball. Set your body perpendicular to the slope so that you effectively give yourself a level lie. Put more of your weight on your right foot and keep it there throughout the swing, as this swing key prevents you from falling forward.

Make a compact backswing. On the downswing, let the club's arc follow the steep slope. Be sure, too, to rotate the right hand under the left, as Tiger does here, to help you keep the clubface wide open—that way the ball will stop fairly quickly once it hits the green.

LEADERS

PRIOR	HOLE	1	2	3	4	5	6	7	8	9	10	11	12	13	14	15	16	17	18
	PAR	4	5	4	3	4	3	4	5	4	4	4	3	5	4	5	3	4	4
15	WOODS	15	16	16	16	15	15	14	15	15	15	16	16	17	18				
6	ROCCA	6	7	7	7	7	6	6	6	6	6	5	5	5	5				
5	STANKOWSKI	5	4	3	2	2	2	3	3	2	3	2	2	2	3	3			
4	KITE T.	4	5	5	4	4	3	4	5	5	5	5	5	6	6	5			
4	WATSON. T.	5	6	6	6	7	6	3	4	4	5	5	6	6	6	6	5		
3	SLUMAN	3	3	3	3	2	2	3	3	3	3	3	3	4	5	3	3		
1	LOVE	0	1	0	0	1	0	0	0	0	0	0	1	3	3	4	3	3	
2	LANGER	2	1	2	2	2	2	1	0	1	0	0	0	1	1	2	2	2	2
2	COUPLES	2	3	3	3	2	1	2	2	2	2	2	2	3	1	1	2	3	
0	TOLLES	0	1	2	2	2	2	2	1	2	2	2	2	3	3	4	5	5	5

THE RIGHT PRESWING PREPARATION

Among the pros on the PGA Tour, Tiger is the most diligent when preparing to hit a chip. Amateurs, who tend to rush their routine and play their favorite club no matter what the situation, can learn a lot from Tiger.

Here Tiger is looking at the terrain and the line to the hole while working his right hand back and through. This preswing procedure allows him to pick the right club and match the speed of swing to the distance of the shot.

THE RUNNING CHIP

Here Tiger plays a running chip from behind the second green at Augusta National, site of the 1997 Masters. He plays this shot much like a putt, taking a square to slightly open stance and keeping his wrists locked while controlling the virtual straight-back straight-through swinging action with his arms and shoulders. As you can see, Tiger also chokes down a couple of inches on the handle for added control.

WHEN A 3-WOOD WORKS BETTER THAN A WEDGE

One of the more funky lies to face is when the ball sits down in the heavier second cut of fringe and there's very little green between the ball and the hole. The natural tendency here is to reach for a wedge, swing back on a steep plane, and hit down sharply. This technique is not the best. Because blades of grass inevitably get stuck between the ball and clubface at impact, the shot flies farther, running well by the hole. A better club for the job is a 3-wood, as Tiger proves practically every time he plays.

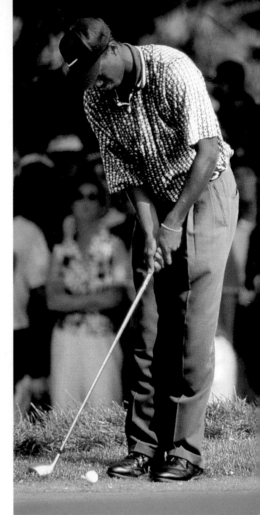

In setting up for this shot, play the ball back in a very narrow stance, putting 70 percent of your weight on your left foot.

Make a very short backswing but let your right wrist hinge a little to set the club on a slightly upright plane.

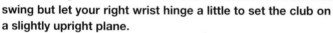

Coming down, delay the unhinging action until impact so that you make contact with the ball using a hit-and-hold action.

As you can see, the ball pops up softly out of the heavy fringe, then begins rolling forward like a purely struck putt. The reason the ball didn't fly off the clubface is that Tiger minimized the flier effect by hitting the ball only slightly on the descent. Try this shot yourself, in practice. I think you'll be surprised how easy it is to play.

THE VALUE OF PRACTICE

One reason why Tiger is so versatile around the greens is that he practices so hard, always teaching himself new shots or perfecting his old, faithful chipping techniques. Tiger has always been conscientious about practice, particularly during his college days at Stanford when he was preparing for the PGA tour.

Here, for example, Tiger is practicing out of what is sometimes called "hay," or wild growing straw-type rough around the greens. Do your game some good: Instead of banging out several buckets of balls with a driver, spend some time chipping out of bad lies.

THE SHORT SAND SHOT (JUST PRIOR TO IMPACT)

Here is Tiger in action, a split second before impact, hitting a short shot out of one of Winged Foot Golf Club's deep, high-lipped bunkers. He's doing what all good sand players do at this point in the swing: keeping his eyes focused intently on a spot a couple of inches behind the ball, where the club will contact the sand. Your lesson: Don't peek.

THE SHORT SAND SHOT (JUST AFTER IMPACT)

Tiger hits the perfect shot. Notice how the divot mark in the sand points left of the flag, proving that Tiger swung across the ball, imparting some left-to-right sidespin on the ball.

To ensure that you make the right swing and hit the right shot, set up completely open and swing your arms and the club along your body line.

THE DIG-DOWN-DEEP SHOT

When the ball is buried in a high-lipped greenside bunker and you have only a little bit of green to work with, you have no choice but to dig out more sand under the ball. To help you hit the best possible shot, assume a very strong grip, open the face of your sand wedge as wide as possible, play the ball up in an exaggerated open stance, make a short backswing, and then swing down, under, and through the ball as forcefully as possible, just like Tiger does here.

THE LONG BUNKER SHOT

To play a long sand shot well, take a very wide closed stance like Tiger's, since this starting position promotes a bigger arc of swing and a flatter action. Additionally, strive for a more low-and-around follow-through, like the one employed here by Tiger, so that you take a longer and thinner slice of sand and hit the ball lower.

PUTTING

THE IMPORTANCE OF A STEADY HEAD

When you set up to putt, make sure that your eyes are either over the ball or over the target line, since either position will help you make a straight-back straight-through stroke. It is also critical that you keep your head steady during the stroke, since even the slightest movement can cause the putter to move off the correct path.

Butch Harmon, realizing the importance of a steady head, works with Tiger on the practice green, regularly checking his setup position, and keeping close tabs on whether he keeps his head in the right position—at the address and during the stroke.

PRACTICING SHORT PUTTS

When practicing short putts, take note of your tendencies. For example, if putts consistently slide off to the right, check your alignment. If that's okay, simply stroke the putt more firmly, keeping the club moving lower and longer along the target line through impact, as Tiger does here on his second putt.

PRACTICING LONG PUTTS

Correctly judging the speed of the green is much more important on long putts. What Tiger does, during practice, is putt balls across the surface of the green. By not aiming at a cup, he takes the pressure off himself to hole out. He therefore is better able to concentrate harder on the speed of the green and its effect on the roll of the ball.

A REASON FOR CELEBRATING

Putting well has a lot to do with your degree of confidence.
So when holing a clutch putt—long or short—don't be afraid
to clench your fist and celebrate. It will raise your level
of confidence and that confidence will filter through the
other departments of your game, making for better shots
and better scores.

What to Do When the Ball Sits Up Too High

The ball is sitting well up on a tuft of grass by the green. The pin is 60 feet away. You are confused about what to do.

What you don't want to do is use a wedge in this situation, since that will cause you to hit the grass under the ball and send it flying only a couple of yards—or feet! Instead, play a six iron.

Play the ball opposite your left heel and take a square stance by aiming your feet, knees, hips, and shoulders parallel to the target line. Snuggle up very close to the ball, as you normally would to putt. Stand virtually erect, with very little flex in your knees, to encourage a low-back low-through stroke. Set the clubhead level with the ball, with its face dead square to the hole.

Make a short, wristless backswing. Next, swing the club through along the target line with your arms, while keeping your head steady. The ball will fly low and run to the hole.

CHIPPING DRILLS

DRILL #1 (For Learning How to Play a Level Stroke)

Many amateur golfers have difficulty hitting a running chip because they allow their wrists to hinge dramatically on the backswing, then hit down too steeply. In order to promote a level through swing, the club must be brought back low to the ground and along the target line during the takeaway. If you hit fat chips, work on the following drill:

1. Place a ball along the target line, about a foot behind the one you intend to hit toward the hole.

2. Swing the club straight back along the target line, keeping your eyes focused on the front ball and your head and body still. The idea is to make a smooth, low takeaway, so that you brush the back ball away.

3. Groove this action through steady practice, then incorporate it into your chip stroke.

DRILL #2 (For Helping You Judge Distance Better)

The typical club-level player hits chip shots either very long or very short of the hole. If this is your problem, the following drill will allow you to develop good eye-hand coordination. As a result, you'll see a big improvement in your distance control.

1. Take your normal chipping setup, placing the club-face of any chipping club squarely behind the ball and perpendicular to a hole some 25 feet away.

2. Next, turn your head and look at the hole. Maintain that head position and make a smooth chip stroke. Hit about ten chips with a few irons, each time watching how the ball reacts in the air and on the ground.

3. Now, revert back to your normal address, keeping your eyes on the ball. Hit the same number of shots with the same clubs. You'll see how much better your distance control is.

DRILL #3 (For Helping You Hit Your Landing Spot)

When playing a lofted chip with a wedge you must carry the ball almost all the way to the hole. The secret to hitting the ball within easy one-putt range is landing the ball on a preselected spot located just short of the hole and in line with it.

To improve your touch, lay out a few small, white dish towels at different distances on your backyard lawn. Now, try to hit each towel.

When playing the course, imagining a dish towel will help you hit spot-on chips.

DRILL #4 (For Improving Your Swing Plane)

Some club-level golfers hit fat chip shots because they let their elbows fly far away from their bodies on the backswing. This fault can cause you to swing on an exaggerated upright plane and hit down too sharply.

To ensure that you swing the club on a flatter plane and hit a controlled running chip, put a headcover under your right armpit. Make your backswing, trying to keep your right elbow tucked close to your body. If the headcover falls out, let your elbow fly. Keep practicing until you groove the correct backswing action.

DRILL #5 (For Correcting a Faulty Swing Path)

I've noticed that many amateur players mishit chip shots because they swing the club too far outside or inside the target line.

If you go through a round either pulling or pushing chips, you share their problem. Here's how to correct it:

1. Place two clubs down on the ground, one on each side of the ball. You want the shafts to be about 3 inches away from the ball and parallel to the target line.

2. Make your stroke. If you hit the shaft farthest from you, you are taking the club too far outside the target line. If you hit the other shaft, you are taking the club too far inside the target line.

3. Keep making backswings until you can make ten consecutive swings without hitting the shafts.

DRILL #6 (For Releasing Tension)

One of the more common faults among amateur golfers is that they freeze over the ball. Thinking too much at address or giving yourself too much time to succumb to a pressure situation can cause your muscles to tense up. There's no way you can hit good chip shots when your muscles are tight, so work on this drill taught to me by veteran Alabama-based teacher Conrad Rehling:

1. Place twenty balls around the chipping green or in your backyard.

2. Start the drill by walking up to the first ball, stepping into the shot, then employing your chip stroke a split second later.

3. Continue on, each time taking note how your arms, hands, hips, wrists, shoulders—and club—move.

This drill will get you out of the thinking mode so that in no time your problem of standing too long over the ball and tensing up will be ancient history.

3

SAND PLAY MAGIC

Knowing on what path to swing the club and how far to hit behind the ball are critical links to playing basic and more sophisticated sand shots like Tiger.

When it comes to sand play, recreational golfers don't realize how easy it would be to recover if they just used a specialized setup and swing. Because most players try to swing normally, they mishit the ball. Others, who think that sand shots are shots only pros can play, either try to pick the ball cleanly out of the sand and send it flying into the lip, or hit down as if they're digging to China, leaving the ball in the bunker.

What makes matters worse is that, in reading the results of a recent survey conducted by *GOLF Magazine,* I learned that many golfers don't carry a sand wedge. If you don't have a sand wedge in your bag, go out and buy one, because in addition to this club's high degree of loft, a special design feature called "bounce" makes it relatively easy for you to recover from sand.

The bounce is a rounded area of flange, below the club's leading edge, that allows the club to slide through the sand more easily.

In working on the book *The Four Cornerstones of Winning Golf,* Butch Harmon explained to me the chief advantages of hitting a lofted sand shot with a sand wedge rather than a pitching wedge. Because the sand wedge's bounce acts like a rudder, you can normally hit a spot approximately 3 inches behind the ball. You don't have to be exact. There's room for error with the sand wedge. On the other hand, if you had to play this same shot with a pitching wedge you would have to contact a precise area of sand very close to the ball. In such a situation, you run the risk of contacting the ball's top half with the wedge's leading edge and hitting an extralow shot that never carries the lip.

The fat bounce area below the club's leading edge is what helps lift the sand—and ball—out of the bunker.

I become frustrated watching golfers treat sand play as a lottery—using the wrong club and swing and hoping that, somehow, the ball will find the green. Of course, you can play this way, too, but a more sensible strategy would be to learn how Tiger Woods approaches this shot and plays it so proficiently. Frankly, learning to be a good sand player will be quite an easy process if you use him as your model. I say that because, as you'll see, Tiger adheres to a very calculated, logical preswing process that readies him for the sand shot he's about to play, plus raises his level of confidence. Additionally, his swing method is much easier to learn and repeat, owing mainly to its simplicity, but also to its naturalness.

Before Tiger even steps into the bunker, he takes a look at the lie, the height of the lip, the distance to the hole, and the slopes and speed of the green. That's because he realizes that, since every situation is slightly different, each shot must be carefully thought out.

Once Tiger analyzes the sand situation, he often practices the swing by hitting the grass outside it with the bounce of the club. He does this for a couple of reasons:

1. It is against the rules to ground your club in sand, or take a practice swing and hit the sand.
2. He wants to get a feel for the length and speed of swing, plus determine how he is going to bring the bounce of the sand wedge into a spot behind the ball.

Remember, when hitting sand shots, the club does not come into direct contact with the ball. You slap the sand behind the ball, slide the club through the sand under the ball, and lift the sand into the air. The late renowned teacher Dick Aultman of the *Golf Digest* pro panel hit the sand behind the ball with a rake to prove to his students that it's the sand that lifts the ball into the air.

This image of the sand lifting the ball out of the bunker, with a magic-carpet effect, will encourage you to fearlessly hit a spot behind the ball.

Once in the bunker, Tiger wriggles his feet into the sand to feel its texture. It's important to do this so that you know how far to hit behind the ball. For example, out of dry, light sand you can hit farther behind the ball because the clubhead will slide quite easily under it. When playing a shot from heavier wet sand you must hit closer behind the ball. This preswing procedure also allows Tiger to establish the firm footing that's needed to stay balanced and swing rhythmically.

Let's now look at the creative ways Tiger plays long and short bunker shots.

The Long Bunker Shot

A sand shot of over 20 yards is considered the toughest shot in golf. However, it doesn't have to be, provided you give up trying to play it out of an open stance and swinging so hard that you lose your balance.

Tiger plays this shot out of an extrawide closed stance, with the ball a few inches behind his left heel, so that he swings on a flatter plane and takes less sand. Consequently, he doesn't need to make as long or fast a swing.

In addition to dropping his right foot back a few inches farther from the target line to promote a more rounded swing, Tiger assumes an extrastrong grip, with the Vs of his thumbs and forefingers pointing just past his right shoulder. This unorthodox grip will feel much more natural to you than the superweak grip you are probably now using. Besides, when you use the stronger right-hand grip, the right arm sits in back of the left, thereby encouraging you to swing the club farther inside the target line. Bernhard Langer, a superb bunker player and Masters champion in 1985 and 1993, realizes the benefits of this unique hold. He once told me that this grip is what allows him to take a shallow cut of sand and send the ball flying all the way to the hole.

Another important element of Tiger's address concerns the width of his stance. He spreads his feet much wider apart than his shoulders to promote a wide arc of swing. This allows him to make a compact swing, yet have plenty of power to propel the ball to the hole. Golfers who take a very narrow stance—spreading their feet only about a foot apart—usually swing the club on a narrow arc going back and coming down. As a result, they shove the club down too deeply into the sand and the shot lacks the strength to carry the lip.

Tiger places about 60 percent of his weight on his right foot, to encourage a good shift into his right side and a more powerful turning action. When you set more weight on your left foot, you tend to swing the club on a narrow arc, which is okay for short bunker shots, but not long ones. Additionally, Tiger points his right foot outward, away from the target line slightly, to further promote a flat swing. The flat swing plane will allow him to take a more shallow cut of sand and fly the ball all the way to the hole, with it biting the split second it hits the green.

On the backswing, Tiger turns his shoulders about 75 degrees, his hips about 25 degrees. He rotates his head away from the target to further encourage a good turning and shifting action of the body. Tiger's backswing ends when his left arm is parallel to the ground and the club reaches the halfway point. Again, he makes a short swing, but by pushing his hands well past his body, he creates a wide, powerful arc of swing. There is no wasted effort.

When Tiger plays a long sand shot, he allows his head to rotate away from the target, as this enhances the turning action of his shoulders.

On the downswing, Tiger generates high clubhead speed through his lower body. First, he slides his knees, legs, and hips laterally toward the target. Once weight shifts to the inside of his left foot, he starts clearing his left hip. This powerful "shift and rotate action," as teacher Jim McLean calls it, helps Tiger accelerate the clubhead through the sand. More important, it discourages him from making a mistake common to many club-level players: releasing the hands too early, and throwing the clubhead deep into the sand. Tiger's good lower body action enables him to maintain the hinge in his wrists until impact, when the wrists snap the club back into, then through, the sand. His follow-through action is low and around, proving that he swung the club on the correct flat plane.

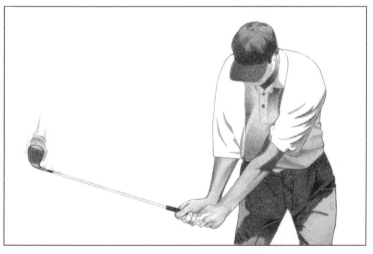

On long bunker shots, clubhead acceleration is highly critical to propelling the ball to the hole.

The Short Bunker Shot

Many bunker shots you face during a round will be from the 10-yard range, with the ball sitting on the surface of the sand behind a relatively high lip. Here, it's necessary to get the ball up very quickly so that it carries the lip, then lands softly before trickling to the hole.

The preswing procedure Tiger follows is basically the same as the one he uses for other bunker shots. His setup, however, is in sharp contrast to the one he uses to play long bunker shots. The upright swing he employs will seem even more natural than the technique for the long bunker shot. That's because it caters to most of our instincts to swing the club up steeply, then unhinge the wrists early on the downswing. This technique will work fine for you, provided that you turn your right hand under your left in the hitting area. I stress the importance of this movement because it is what allows you to hit a high, more controlled sand shot.

Tiger plays the ball forward in an open stance, off his left heel normally, but off his left instep if the ball is very close to the lip and the distance to the hole is under 10 yards. Playing the ball up in the stance allows you to contact the sand at the bottom of the swing's arc, with the club sliding fluidly through it. Standing open, like Tiger, with your right foot a few inches closer to the target line and perpendicular to it, will promote the ideal upright swing. To further ensure that you swing the club more up than around, narrow your stance, set approximately 60 percent of your weight on the left foot, and turn your hands toward the target, so that the Vs formed by your thumbs and forefingers point up at your left ear.

When gripping, hold the club lightly to encourage active hand-wrist action. Also, choke down on the club a couple of inches to compensate for digging your feet more deeply into the sand.

Regarding the position of the club, the shorter the shot and the closer you are to the lip, the more you should lay the face open. Generally, you should open the clubface the same number of degrees you align your body to the left. For the short shot being discussed here, Tiger opens his feet and clubface about 25 degrees.

Open the clubface when playing a short sand shot over a high lip.

In taking the club back, Tiger leaves the majority of his weight on his left foot and hinges his wrists very early in the takeaway. The club never swings behind him; in fact, when he's really looking to hit a high, short, quick-stopping shot, he pushes the club well outside the target line as a way of getting himself in position to put added

In playing the short bunker shot, swing the club back short of the parallel position, along your open body line.

cut-spin on the ball. In such cases, he sets his hands behind the ball at address; normally, you want to line your hands up with the ball and swing the club back parallel to your body line.

The backswing itself is compact, but much more upright than the one used to play a long bunker shot. The arc must be steep in order to explode the ball out of the sand.

Coming down, Tiger swings the club across the target line. He uncocks his right wrist practically at the start of the downswing and also rotates his right hand under his left to help him maintain the open clubface position through impact. This timed wrist-hand action allows Tiger to slap the sand with the bounce of the club. The other elements of a good downswing are accelerating the arms and finishing high. Both of these keys promote a lofted, soft-landing shot.

Tiger's left-arm chicken-wing position encourages him to swing across the target line.

TROUBLE SHOTS:
HOW TO RECOVER LIKE TIGER

How to Handle a Buried Lie

This shot calls for a digging rather than a sliding action of the club through the sand. Therefore, you need to choose a pitching wedge, featuring a sharper leading edge than the sand wedge, and less bounce, too.

You will also need to make a very steep swing. To encourage this type of plane, play the ball close to the midpoint in your stance, with your hands well ahead. Set the clubface square to the ball and hole, and guard against pulling the ball left of target by assuming a square stance and body alignment. Also, set about 70 percent of your weight on your left foot. To further foster an exaggerated upright plane of swing, bend over more at the waist and tilt your knees and hips toward the target slightly.

The backswing action should be controlled entirely with the arms and hands. Pick the club practically straight up into the air, leaving your lower body locked in the address position.

Let your hands lead the downswing. Pull the club down into a spot about an inch behind the ball, a half inch if you have plenty of green to work with. Because you should use a sharp hit-and-hold action to bring the club into the sand, the follow-through will be extra-short.

In a normal buried lie situation, play a pitching wedge, and contact the sand approximately 1 inch behind the ball.

How to Deal with Slopes

In hitting these shots, remember the following three keys used by Tiger:

1. At address, let the angle of your body match the angle of the slope.
2. Play the ball opposite your higher foot.
3. Swing along the slope.

What to Do When the Ball Is Close to the Bunker's Back Lip

Play the ball just behind the midpoint of your stance, with your hands well ahead of it. Brace your right leg to

---

avoid swaying. If you sway your body on the backswing, the club is likely to hit the lip. Here's what you do:

1. Lay the clubface wide open.

2. Swing the club back on an exaggerated upright plane.

3. Pull the club down sharply, contacting the sand about 1½ inches behind the ball, and take a much deeper cut.

When the ball lies close to the bunker's back lip, hit closer to the ball than normal and let the club make a deeper cut into the sand.

What to Do When the Ball Is in Sand and One Foot Is Out of the Bunker

Sometimes, the lie is such that the best you can do is stand with one foot out of the bunker to hit the shot. The key to hitting this shot is staying down, so increase the flex in your knees.

It is also important that you don't rock your body on the backswing or let your lower body become over-active on the downswing. You want to swing the club with your hands and arms, so encourage good hand and arm action by gripping the club very lightly.

On the way down, focus intently on your contact spot in the sand, since that will encourage you to stay down and swing the club fluidly through the ball.

What to Do When the Sand Is Packed Down

The simple secrets to success are playing the ball 2 inches behind your left heel, opening the face of a pitching wedge, swinging the club back outside the target line, and hitting a half inch behind the ball using a hit-and-stop action.

SAND PLAY DRILLS

DRILL #1 (For Determining the Best Wedge for Your Course)

In different parts of the country, the texture of the sand varies. Most often, you'll be hitting out of semisoft sand, with an underbase that offers some resistance. From this kind of sand, a sand wedge with 10 to 14 degrees of bounce works best.

In very soft sand, you must guard against digging down too deeply. A sand wedge that features more than 14 degrees of bounce works best.

In firm sand, use a wedge with less than 10 degrees of bounce; otherwise the club is likely to bounce into the ball, with a top resulting.

Check with your pro to see if you have the right wedge for the sand on your course.

DRILL #2 (For Learning How to Take a Shallow Cut of Sand)

The reason Tiger hits such good long bunker shots is because he swings on a flat plane and takes such a shallow cut of sand. Conversely, amateurs pick the club up too quickly, then chop down. This drill, taught to me by guru teacher Jim McLean—who learned it from former Tour pro Al Mengert—will train you to take a shallow cut of sand:

1. Make some light footprints in the sand.

2. Swinging a sand wedge, try to brush through the length of the footprint, erasing it.

3. Make some new footprints, only this time put a ball in the center of them.

4. Again, try to erase each footprint.

Bring this image to the course, and I guarantee you'll play better long bunker shots.

DRILL #3 (For Grooving a Compact Swing)

When playing a long bunker shot, Tiger also keeps his backswing compact. You should, too, because if you swing beyond parallel you run the risk of overcocking the wrists. This fault will usually cause you to unhinge the wrists too early on the downswing and throw the club down too deeply into the sand. As a result, the ball stays in the bunker or, at best, falls well short of the hole.

To help you groove a compact swing, pretend that there is a clock around your body. Your head is 12 o'clock; a point midway between your feet is 6 o'clock. As you practice long bunker shots, try to swing your hands to the 3 o'clock position. Get used to the feeling and you will hit the ball the right distance consistently.

DRILL #4 (For Learning to Hold the Clubface Open, through Impact, on a Short Bunker Shot)

When Tiger was growing up and learning golf, his father used to present him with some tough course situations, and even use gamesmanship against him. Instead of Tiger's becoming intimidated, he became tougher.

The next time you practice sand shots, spend some time making things tough on yourself. Throw about twenty balls in a bunker and try to hit short shots with a five iron. This drill will teach you the importance of opening up the clubface, swinging back along your open body line, and swinging through across the target line while staying behind the ball.

When you finish practicing these shots, throw another twenty balls down and see how easy it now is to recover with a sand wedge.

DRILL #5 (For Learning How to Control Distance)

How far behind the ball the club contacts the sand greatly influences the distance you hit the shot. Generally, the closer your contact point is to the ball the less sand you take and the farther you will hit the ball.

To be a good sand player who can play a variety of shots, you must learn to make contact at different points behind the ball. Here's a drill to help you control distance as well as Tiger does, taught to me by teacher Jim Gerber, one of *GOLF Magazine*'s 100 best teachers in America:

1. In a practice bunker, draw a grid with the lines 10 inches apart and put balls in the center (leaving 5 inches of sand in both the front and back of the ball).

2. Go from one section to the next, hitting 3 inches behind the ball. If you swung down and through correctly, there will be a 2-inch gap of sand be-

tween the back line and where the club entered the sand, and a 2-inch gap between the front line and where the club left the sand.

3. To become more versatile, draw two new grids, one for hitting 2 inches behind the ball, the other for 1 inch. (You'll rarely have to hit just 1 inch behind the ball, but it's better to be prepared.)

DRILL #6 (To Learn the Feeling of Using the Club's Bounce)

To hit the ball over a high lip and spin it, you must accelerate the sand wedge through impact. Even on short bunker shots, you don't want the club's leading edge to dig too deeply into the sand. Ideally, you must slap the ground with the bounce of the club. In order to familiarize yourself with the proper through-impact actions, hit shots out of cushioned lies in the grass. Each time, hit a spot in the grass about 2 inches behind the ball and listen for the sound of the bounce making contact with the ground. Practicing this technique in grass rather than in sand will be less intimidating, since you will not feel the pressure of hitting the ball close to the cup.

Once you learn the correct slapping action, practice hitting shots out of a bunker. You'll see immediately that your unorthodox practice was well worth it.

DRILL #7 (For Learning the Correct Follow-Through Actions)

Tiger Woods is a very imaginative player, using mental images to help himself. Gary Player, another expert on bunker shots, has done this throughout his career. Here's a drill he taught me that is sure to help you with your sand game:

1. Place two stakes in the sand, with a rope tied quite loosely from one to the other. The rope should be level with your chest.

2. Place a ball a couple of feet behind the stakes—on your side of the fence, so to speak.

3. Set up to play a short bunker shot. Swing. If your club contacts the rope, it means you accelerated through impact and swung into a nice high follow-through position.

4. Next, set up to play a short bunker shot out of a buried lie. Swing. If you correctly used a hit-and-stop action through impact, the club should not have contacted the rope.

Keep these short and long follow-through images in your head when you play the course.

4

PUTTING MAGIC

Learning Tiger's pure pendulum stroke will help you sink more long, short, and curling putts.

The hardest thing about putting is dealing with the contradictions. The putting green looks as smooth as a billiard table's top, and the putting stroke itself is far simpler and shorter than what's used to play other clubs, yet putting remains the trickiest department of the game. The ironies do not stop there. The truth is, putting greens are not nearly as smooth as they look. Putting expert and former NASA physicist Dave Pelz proved that tiny imperfections in the green, plus spike marks and small incorrectly repaired ball divots, can keep a well-stroked putt out of the hole or cause a poorly struck putt to fall into the cup. So, the element of luck enters the picture, at least to some degree. The stroke is not that simple, either—a slight misalignment of the putterface or a small mistake in the stroke is all it takes for the ball to miss the 4¼-inch-wide hole.

Average players and PGA Tour professionals alike realize the mysterious side to putting. They wonder why on some days they miss putts on the practice green before a round, then go out and make practically everything on the course, and why on other days they hole putt after putt in practice, then miss everything in play. They wonder why they can sometimes stand over a putt, a long winding one at that, and know they are going to hole it, and why, on other occasions, they suddenly start thinking negatively about missing an easy 2-foot straight-in putt, then do just that. What really baffles them, though, is how some hackers they know can putt as well as, or better than, they can.

Putting is such a here-one-day-and-gone-the-next thing that it drives golfers crazy. That's why players constantly change putters, putting grips, stances, and styles of stroke. On the whole, however, these golfers who never stick with one thing long enough to learn how it works are the ones who will never master the art of putting.

Although Tiger, with the help of coach Butch Harmon, has made minor tweaks to his setup and stroke, he sticks to a pure pendulum action, controlled by the arms and shoulders—not the wrists—because he knows in his head and his heart that this method is the one that will work best the longest.

Not that all of Tiger's days on the greens are great. Granted, en route to winning the 1997 Masters he made more than his share of par, birdie, and eagle putts, and even more impressive, he went around the seventy-two holes at Augusta National without three-putting once. But juxtaposed with this sensational performance were Tiger's bad putting scores at the '97 PGA and Ryder Cup.

Still, no matter how bad things get, Tiger sticks to the same putter, a Scotty Cameron Titleist model. According to Butch Harmon, Tiger doesn't believe in blaming the club for missed putts. As the saying goes, "It's not the putter, it's the puttee."

Tiger also sticks to the same preswing routine, realizing that no matter how good a putter feels in your hands, and no matter how good your stroke, if you fail to read the break in the green correctly or incorrectly line your body and the putterface up to the hole, you will never be a consistently good putter.

Tiger's Preswing Routine

Once arriving on the green, Tiger stalks the putt, carefully analyzing the slopes from all angles to determine which way the ball will break.

Commenting on Tiger's routine, Jim McLean said this to me: "Tiger, like all great putters, relishes the moment when it's his turn to putt. He executes his routine with supreme confidence. The green is his stage and, like a great actor, he takes charge."

It's critical that you follow a similar process, being sure to: *Get a bird's-eye view of the line from behind the cup, looking back to the ball; view the putt from both side angles; look at the putt from behind the ball.*

If Tiger is unsure of the break, he will plumb-bob the line. This is how that procedure works.

Stand behind the ball, with your body perpendicular to the horizon. Hold the putter at arm's length in front of you, with only your right thumb and forefinger securing the top of the grip and the clubshaft hanging vertically. Line up so the shaft covers the ball, then close your nondominant eye. If the clubshaft now covers the hole, there is no break in the green; the putt is dead straight. If the clubshaft appears to be left of the hole, the putt will break from left to right. If the clubshaft appears to be right of the hole, the plumb bob indicates that the putt will break from right to left.

Tiger and other top pros know only too well that it's not enough to be able to correctly judge the line of a putt. Like Johnny Miller, who was a great putter in his heyday, Tiger pays close attention to the grain, or the direction in which the blades of grass grow, since it affects the roll of the ball. To read the grain, crouch down with the sun at your back and look at the grass along your intended line. If the grass has a sheen to it, you know that the grain is with you, signaling a faster putt. A dull look means the grain is against you, and that thus you can expect the ball to roll more slowly.

Grain is more prevalent on the Bermuda grass greens of the South and Southwest. Nevertheless, all strains of grass grow toward bodies of water near the green, meaning the putt will almost always break in the same direction.

Tiger's last look at the line of a putt is from behind the ball, almost always in the presence of his caddie.

Tiger's last look is from behind the ball, usually in the company of his caddie. Once they agree on the line, Tiger starts to swing his putter back and forth, sometimes with just his right hand, to get a feel for how hard to stroke the putt. Finally, he stares intently down the line, giving his confidence level a positive lift by envisioning the ball rolling toward the hole and dropping into the cup.

Tiger's Putting Grip

Take one look at the pros putting on the practice green before starting a tournament round, and you'll realize that putting grips vary. For example, Craig Stadler points his right forefinger straight down behind the shaft, so that he can more easily guide the putter back and through along the target line. John Daly crooks his right forefinger under the shaft. Bernhard Langer feels more secure grasping both the clubshaft and his left forearm with his right hand. The list goes on.

Tiger himself is quite unorthodox, using a variation of the popular reverse-overlap grip used by many great putters over the years. Instead of overlapping his left forefinger over his right pinkie, he lets it drape over the last two fingers of his left hand. Jack Nicklaus uses the identical grip. This hold prevents the wrists from hinging on the backswing and downswing. Therefore, Tiger is better able to swing the putter back low to the ground and on the correct path, which for short putts is straight back and straight through; on long putts, from inside the

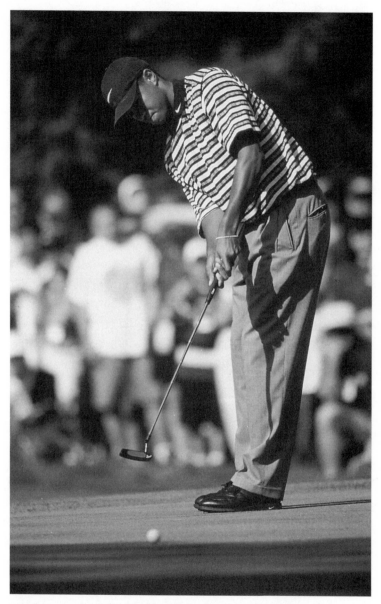

Tiger's unusual grip, shared by Jack Nicklaus, helps him keep his wrists quiet during the stroke.

target line on the backswing, to square at impact, to inside the target line in the follow-through. But I'm getting ahead of myself. Let's first analyze Tiger's setup position.

Tiger's Setup

Tiger normally positions the ball 1 to 2 inches inside his left heel, which is the lowest point in the stroke. He balances his weight evenly on the central part of each foot to preserve the best sense of balance. His hands line up with the ball, since that position promotes a level back-and-through stroke. If your hands drift ahead of the ball, the tendency is to pick the putter up into the air on the backswing, then chop down at impact. If you line up with your hands behind the ball, you will tend to swing the putter back outside the target line, then cut across it going through.

Normally, Tiger sets his feet, knees, hips, and shoulders parallel to the target line to promote the best possible on-line stroke. However, to give himself a clearer view of an awkward uphill putt, or when putting a left-to-right breaking putt, Tiger will set his body just slightly open to the target line, or a bit left of the parallel position. In aligning the putterface, he always sets it down squarely behind the ball, with its sweetspot perpendicular to the hole.

Something else that Tiger pays close attention to is the position of his head. Butch Harmon monitors Tiger's setup frequently, checking to see that he keeps his eyes directly over the ball. Harmon maintains that this further encourages you to make an on-line stroke, and I agree with him, especially since putting expert and two-time PGA champion Paul Runyan said that oculists had

A good part of Tiger's putting practice focuses on grooving a good setup position.

informed him that this starting position makes it easier to see the straight putting line. Still, you may want to experiment to see if you putt better with your eyes behind the ball and over the target line. Many good putters, such as Jack Nicklaus, putt this way.

The thing you don't want to do on short putts is set your eyes over an area well inside the target line. This position will encourage you to swing the putter so far inside the target line—on an overly flat path—that you will have difficulty squaring up the clubface. Besides, as Dave Pelz told me: "The easiest path of the putter to duplicate is the straight-back straight-through stroke, simply because the putterhead never leaves the path that runs along your target line."

Something else Tiger pays close attention to is the position of his hands. Just prior to the final round of the 1998 Johnnie Walker Classic, in Thailand, Earl Woods told his son that he was swinging on an exaggerated flat path and missing short putts because his hands were too low and far from his body. Heeding his father's advice to move his hands up and in, Tiger shot a sixty-five in the last round, coming from eight shots back to win the title.

Just before Tiger strokes the putt he pauses to take a couple of breaths. According to Jim McLean, in Japan these are known as *Zazen* breaths. You inhale through the nose and the mouth. Breath control calms the nerves and fosters great concentration.

The Putting Stroke. Like many of the pros, Tiger has toyed with various strokes, including trying a wristy action in late 1997 when he was suffering a putting slump. Tiger quickly discovered, however, that such a stroke is harder to repeat and depends greatly on perfect timing. If you hinge the wrists in the backswing, then unhinge them early in the downswing, the tendency is to pull putts, or to top the ball and send it flying well past

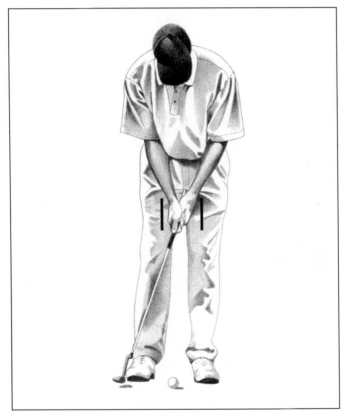

On the greens, Tiger concentrates intently on employing an arms-shoulders-controlled pendulum stroke.

the hole. In fact, the latter fault caused Tiger to knock a putt off the green and into the water during the 1997 Ryder Cup matches. If you unhinge the wrists too late, the tendency is to push putts.

The type of stroke Tiger depends on is a wristless pendulum-style back-and-through action. And there's nothing fancy about it. The simple secret to repeating this no-frills stroke, and keeping the putterface square to the hole, is maintaining a steady head and body position during the backswing and downswing. You want to stay locked in position while only the arms and shoulders swing the putterblade back low to the ground and through low to the ground.

Some amateurs, and pros who are inconsistent putters, have been taught to swing the putterhead upward through impact, believing this will give them a better roll of the ball. One of *GOLF Magazine*'s top 100 teachers, Rick Grayson, has a big problem with this method and wonders how it started being taught in the first place.

Says Grayson, who teaches at the Bill and Payne Stewart Golf Course in Springfield, Missouri: "I discovered that the best way to discourage the ball from skidding or bouncing, and to instead have it start rolling purely, is to keep the putterhead moving low to the ground in the hitting area and for several inches past impact. When Tiger is on, no player does that better than him."

Like all world-class putters, Tiger keeps the clubhead moving low to the ground through impact.

WHICH IS BETTER: A LIGHT OR FIRM GRIP?

I agree with Butch Harmon that grip pressure should be on the firm side. On a scale of 1 to 10, with 1 representing a superlight grip and 10 a superfirm grip, Harmon advocates a pressure of around 7. You want a hold that is firm enough to keep the putter swinging on the correct path, but light enough to help you feel the putterhead. That feel is critical to judging how hard to hit the ball.

As a matter of note, Tiger also points both his thumbs straight down the shaft, in order to help him guide the putter along the target line.

ON LONG PUTTS, SHOULD YOU PULL THE PUTTER INSIDE THE TARGET LINE? SHOULD YOU BREAK YOUR WRISTS?

On longer putts, the backswing should be longer and the putter should swing inside the target line. However, let the clockwise rotation of the shoulders bring the putter inside automatically. Don't ever consciously pull the putter inside the target line. This backswing fault causes you to swing the putter on such an exaggerated inside path that squaring its face to the ball at impact becomes very difficult indeed. Provided you rotate your shoulders counterclockwise on the downswing, the putterface will be delivered squarely into the ball.

Don't ever purposely break your wrists on the backswing, either. This fault causes you to pick the putter up steeply, then chop down on it. If the wrists hinge naturally due to the swinging weight of the clubhead, that's permissible, especially if your feel is enhanced. Although some pros and teachers advocate a slight wrist hinge on long putts, saying it helps you judge speed, I go along with world-renowned teacher Jim Flick of the Nicklaus-Flick Golf School. He once told me that average golfers should only have one speed producer in putting—the arms, not the wrists and hands.

Tiger has never taken a formal putting lesson from Flick, but he apparently agrees with Flick's philosophy. Tiger uses the big muscles of his arms, rather than the small ones, to propel the ball to the hole. I consider this a smart policy, since it's easier to control the putter with the arms and shoulders than with the hands and wrists.

WHAT TYPE OF PUTTER IS BEST?

Choosing a putter is a very personal thing, so you may or may not like a Titleist putter like Tiger's. There are literally hundreds of models to choose from. The best advice I can give you is to determine which putter looks and feels the best. Ideally you should test a few out on the putting green of your local course. After all, ugly or beautiful, cheap or expensive, the putter you choose must be able to roll the ball into the hole.

It's also important to find a model that features a mark to designate the most solid part of the putterface, its "sweetspot." It doesn't matter if your ideal putter is a brand-new model or one found in an old barrel in a junk shop. As long as it works, it's a great putter. If you find a putter you like but it has no sweetspot marking, here's how to locate it. Lightly grasp the top of the handle with only your thumb and forefinger, letting the putter hang vertically. Next, take a quarter and tap the putterface at different points. When you tap a specific spot and notice that the putter swings to and fro without wobbling, you have discovered the sweetspot. Now, file a marking into the top of the putterhead that lines up with the sweetspot. Finally, paint it in a color that's easily visible. You'll find that this mark will also help you line putts up squarely to the hole.

How to Handle Fringe Grass

When putting over fringe grass, Tiger swings the putter at normal speed, but hits the top half of the ball to impart overspin on it.

Even the smoothest-looking areas of fringe will slow the ball's roll and knock a putt off course. Yet just because the ball lies in the fringe doesn't mean you have to hit the ball harder.

Set up with the putterface's sweetspot square to the top half of the ball. Now, simply make a level back-and-through stroke at normal speed. Hitting the top portion of the ball will impart overspin on it, allowing you to roll it nicely through the fringe with little effect from the uneven grass.

How to Deal with a Steep Downhill Putt

In this situation many amateurs shorten their backswing, then decelerate the putter through impact. As a result, the putt stops short of the downslope, and well short of the cup.

The best strategy is to use your normal-length stroke, but contact the ball toward the toe of the putter to lighten the hit.

How to Deal with a Steep Uphill Putt

Pretend that the putt is longer than it is by imagining a second cup several feet behind the one you're aiming at. This will encourage you to accelerate the putterhead in the hitting area and hit the ball up to the hole.

How to Handle Wet Greens

The secret to sinking putts on slower, wet greens is allowing for half as much break as under dry conditions.

How to Handle Heavy Winds

Unless you normally play golf in Texas or Florida, or make regular trips to Scotland or Ireland, this is an unusual course condition. Still, from time to time, wind will play havoc with your game. In such course conditions, an extrawide stance will help. Top pros and teachers have told me that this wide base gives them the added stability needed to make a controlled stroke.

How to Deal with a Short Pressure Putt

Many amateurs who try to easily coax a putt into the hole on fast greens leave the ball short or allow it to break off line. Take a lesson from Tiger: He almost always rams the ball solidly into the hole, as boldly as Tom Watson did during his heyday.

The next time you face a 3- to 6-foot pressure putt, grip the club a little more firmly than normal so you are more apt to make a pure pendulum stroke. When you grip the putter extralightly, the putterhead moves off the square-to-square path, causing the ball to roll off its intended line.

When analyzing a green featuring varying slope configurations, Tiger points the putter at the hole. I think this better allows him to reference exactly where the ball will start breaking.

Strategies on Breaking Putts

Before even thinking about your stroke you should squat down behind the ball and look at the basic slope of the green. Next, pick out a specific spot on the line to the hole where you believe the ball will start breaking or curving. Aim the putterface at that spot. Now, hit the ball toward it. As to proper technique, here's how to handle left-to-right and right-to-left putts.

When hitting a left-to-right putt, play the ball off your left heel. This forward ball position will encourage the putterface to contact the ball as it's almost closing. You'll keep the ball left of the hole, or on the "high" side. The advantage of keeping the ball on the high side is that it allows it to stop closer to the hole. Putts hit on the low side roll farther away from the hole.

When hitting a right-to-left putt, play the ball off your right heel. This rearward ball position will encourage the putterface to be slightly open at impact, ensuring that the ball stays right of the hole.

How to Handle Baked-Out Greens

If the greens are baked out because of exposure to the sun and wind, the ball will roll faster. You will need to compensate by making a slightly slower stroke than normal.

PUTTING DRILLS

DRILL #1 (For Grooving the Correct Position of the Eyes)

If you consistently push putts right of the hole, your eyes are probably well inside the target line. This position distorts your view of the target and usually causes you to aim the putter to the right. Worse, it causes you to swing the putter back so far to the inside that, at impact, the putterface points farther right of the hole. Here's how to ensure that you're in the ideal starting position:

1. Take your normal putting stance, with the ball played just inside your left heel.

2. Hold a ball next to the bridge of your nose, then drop it. If the ball lands more than an inch inside the target line, change your head position.

3. Repeat this exercise until the ball consistently drops on the one you addressed, or on the target line itself.

DRILL #2 (To Cure a Sway Problem)

Players who start correctly with their eyes over the ball, then sway, get themselves into trouble. The best putters in the world, including Tiger Woods, keep their head and body perfectly still while swinging the putter back and through with their arms and shoulders.

If you move off the ball, it is very difficult to deliver

the putterface squarely to it. If you have this problem, you can lock yourself in position by pointing your right foot perpendicular to the target line and setting up in a sort of "knock-kneed" position. Practice this setup a few times a day, at the course or in your living room, until it becomes natural.

DRILL #3 (For Intensifying Your Concentration)

Players who let their minds drift during preround practice usually hit putts on the course that finish left, right, short, and long of the hole.

To help get your concentration level primed for the course, practice with just one ball instead of throwing three balls down on the green and putting without focus. Following this one-ball practice procedure will intensify your concentration. More important, you'll carry this intense mind-set to the course and see quick improvement in your putting scores.

DRILL #4 (For Relieving Tension)

The player who is tense over the ball usually has difficulty making a pure pendulum stroke using the big muscles of the arms and shoulders. Typically, he or she uses the small muscles of the hands to swing the putter. This makes it difficult to swing the putter on the correct path. To alleviate tension and promote a smooth big-muscle-controlled stroke, hold the putterhead slightly off the ground. Practice this new setup position and slowly incorporate it into your on-course routine.

DRILL #5 (For Helping You Feel the Correct Putting Action)

Many golfers mishit putts because they think too much about the mechanics of the stroke. To help you focus more on feeling the action rather than thinking about it, try whistling as you practice putting.

DRILL #6 (For Helping You Sink More Short Putts)

If you miss several short pressure putts during a round, practice putting at a tee 3 feet away. This drill will make you concentrate so intently on the line and extrasmall target that, when you get to the course, the hole will seem cavernous.

DRILL #7 (For Promoting an Accelerating Stroke)

If you consistently leave putts short of the hole because you decelerate the clubhead in the impact zone and stop at the ball, here's how to fix your fault. Place a quarter about 3 inches in front of the ball. As you hit practice putts, brush the coin with the putterhead. Now, simply incorporate this accelerating follow-through into your technique.

DRILL #8 (For Curing an Overly Wristy Stroke)

The player who overdoes wrist action usually has great difficulty keeping the putterface square to the target line. Moreover, he or she usually hits the ball well by the hole. If this is your problem, practice standing more erect, with your arms hanging down naturally. That way, when you grip the putter the angles will be out of your wrists.

Your new setup will make it easier for you to employ a pure arms-shoulders stroke.

DRILL #9 (For Improving Your Preswing Procedure)

Many golfers miss putts because they read the break incorrectly. One reason is that they tend to rush their preswing routine, only reading a putt from behind the ball. I blame this problem on poor practice habits.

When you practice, train yourself to have good habits by also reading the putt from behind the hole and from both sides of the target line.

DRILL #10 (For Grooving Good Alignment Habits)

You can have the best stroke in the world, but if you align the putterface incorrectly, you've got little chance of holing putts consistently. If you lack confidence in your alignment skills, set down a dozen balls in a straight line, the first one 6 inches from the cup, the others a foot apart.

Because the first four putts are so close to the hole, you should have no problem squaring up the clubface to the target line and holing out. This will make you more confident and encourage you to concentrate even harder as you putt from farther away.

DRILL #11 (For Helping You Become a Better Lag Putter)

On long putts, judging speed correctly is more important than judging line. Tiger realizes this fact, so he works on his distance control by lagging putts from one side of the putting green to points just short of the green's fringe line on the other side. Practice the same drill. Not putting to a hole encourages you to make speed a priority and allows you to pace the ball nicely across the putting surface.

INDEX

About the Author

JOHN ANDRISANI is the consulting editor of *GOLF Magazine* and author of the book *The Tiger Woods Way: An Analysis of Tiger Woods' Power-Swing Technique*. A former golf instructor, Andrisani has coauthored several books with the game's greatest players and major championship winners, including Sandy Lyle, Seve Ballesteros, Fred Couples, and John Daly. He has also written numerous books with the world's top instructors, most notably *The Four Cornerstones of Winning Golf,* which he collaborated on with Claude "Butch" Harmon, Tiger Woods' teacher.

A course record holder and past winner of the World Golf Writers' Championship, Andrisani resides in Orlando, Florida.

About the Photographers

PHIL SHELDON and JAN TRAYLEN are London-based photographers whose work appears in books and golf magazines published around the world.

About the Illustrator

ALLEN WELKIS is an award-winning artist who has worked with major publishing houses, television networks, prominent film studios, leading magazines, and top advertising agencies. An avid golfer, Welkis lives in Fort Salonga, New York.

NOTES